THIS BOOK BELONGS TO

ALEX MOSS-ECCAROT

An Adult Confirmation Candidate's Handbook

Also by CANON RAYMOND WILKINSON:

My Confirmation Search Book

An Adult Confirmation Candidate's Handbook

A SHORT GUIDE TO THE HISTORY, ORGANIZATION, DOCTRINE AND CEREMONIES OF THE CHURCH OF ENGLAND, FOR THOSE NEEDING BASIC INSTRUCTION IN THE FAITH

BY

CANON RAYMOND WILKINSON

Chaplain to H.M. The Queen

FOREWORD BY THE BISHOP OF BIRMINGHAM

MOWBRAY

FIRST PUBLISHED 1964 BY THE FAITH PRESS LTD
THIS 6TH (REVISED) EDITION PUBLISHED 1983
BY MOWBRAY, A CASSELL IMPRINT
VILLIERS HOUSE, 41/47 STRAND
LONDON WC2N 5JE

REPRINTED 1991

ISBN 0 264 66989 4

Printed and bound in Great Britain by
Biddles Ltd, Guildford and King's Lynn

FOREWORD

TODAY an ever-increasing proportion of those coming forward to Confirmation are adults. These are mature people who show their Christian commitment in the Church of England by taking this important step.

The Church however needs not only committed but also instructed lay people, confident of their role because they know where they stand, and because they can give a reason for the faith that is in them.

As the number of priests in the Church continues to decline, the need for trained lay people becomes more urgent so that they can take their full share in non-priestly ministries. It is encouraging that in many parishes and dioceses steps are being taken to provide this.

These people need a 'primer'. Canon Raymond Wilkinson's handbook has already stood the test of time. This revised edition, written by a pastor of wisdom and experience, who has always had a deep concern for education, assembles in readable form what is needed.

I am glad to commend it, and I hope that it will continue to be widely used.

30 May 1983 + HUGH BIRMINGHAM

INTRODUCTION

MANY parish priests nowadays are having the joy of preparing for Confirmation larger classes of adults than ever before. We also find that properly prepared adults bring to the Church an enthusiasm and devotion sometimes lacking in those who have grown up taking the Faith for granted.

The writer has for some years had his talks to adult Confirmation Candidates printed or cyclostyled for members of the group to read at home during the week prior to the class, along with any other research indicated; the chapter, or an appropriate section, is then read aloud at the meeting for all to think about again, and followed with discussion on the lines of the suggested titles given at the end of each chapter.

This book makes a happy method available for others who have the pleasure of leading adult Confirmation Classes, or chairing adult Discussion Groups, where revision on the facts of our Faith is sought.

ACKNOWLEDGEMENT

The greater part of Chapter 5 of this book is taken from *The Gospel-Catechism Lessons* by Norman Campbell, published by SPCK.

CONTENTS

CHAPTER I

Basic Considerations

LIVING A 'GOOD' LIFE

MOST people seem to have the idea that 'being religious' means not being wicked; that a man who is religious is a man who doesn't drink, doesn't swear, doesn't tell unclean stories, doesn't carry on with another man's wife. It is thought, in other words, that religion is a matter of morality—and nothing else.

Let us think of a young man who is a keen athlete. In order to be at his best he gives up smoking. This doesn't mean that people say of him: 'He is an athlete: therefore he doesn't smoke.' If they wish to talk about his athletics, they talk about the things he *does*—his skill, his keenness, his successes. His skill as an athlete does not rest in his not smoking. Plenty of people give up smoking for other reasons, in any case—because they cannot afford it, or because they think it a bad habit, or for health reasons, or because they want to prove to themselves that they can give it up.

The Christian religion, therefore, is not merely a case of living the good life. Plenty of folk live a good life for all sorts of reasons. Some because they fear what will happen to them if they don't; some because they find the good life the most satisfying; some because they think the good life is best for society as a whole. Thousands and thousands of people in the world live good, moral lives; and they are not necessarily 'religious' people.

Christian morality is the outcome of Christian belief. This belief is that we in this world are the children of a personal God who cares, who loves, who redeems—a God who is, therefore, to be worshipped, spoken with, served and obeyed; a God who enters into a relationship with His children, personally and corporately. *Part* of our response to God is that we shall wish to please Him in our lives. This is the basis of Christian behaviour. But the moral response is only *part* of our response. It is the part which follows quite naturally when we have made the response of *faith,* and the response of *prayer* and *worship*—the re-orientation of our daily life which takes place when we have encountered the grace of God in worship.

Put first things first. The man who is religious is the man who tries to live his life in an intimate relationship with the God of Love, in the power of Jesus Christ. His morality is the *fruit* of his religion—not the basis for it.

Further reading:

The Centre of Christianity (Hick, SCM Press).
Ethics and the Christian (David Brown, Blackwells).

Discuss:

How far does what a man believes affect his conduct?

IS SECURITY POSSIBLE?

The deepest need of the human spirit in this world is security. We all need some basis on which our souls can find absolute peace and certainty. Life for many is shallow, restless, futile—because the heart has no abiding centre of rest. The child finds that security in his home, in the affection of father and mother. He may not think very often or very long about their love, but all the time he knows it is there. At the roots of his life is a love he can trust to the uttermost, and on that love he leans. The personal centre of affection and care gives home its right value. Without it no child can develop normally. The lack of it in early life is one of the main causes of trouble in later years.

But in the great world we all need this basis of security. Some try to find it in money. The hunt for wealth that keeps many people toiling, even when they have abundance, is often due to this craving for security.

The rich fool in the parable had this in mind when he thought of his barns filled to capacity—'Soul, take thine ease.' In other words—'You have no need to worry about anything.' Our Lord called him foolish because he did not see that there are things against which money is no security. It cannot secure us against sorrow, sickness or death.

There is only one basis of security—the love of God. Only the Eternal can give real peace to the spirit in a material world. Like the child, we need a personal centre of care and wisdom to lean upon. Nothing less will serve. The lack of it is indeed the root of all our loneliness, as one has seen so often in those suffering from mental breakdown. That great and original genius, Dr. Carl Jung, to whom many thousands turned in such distress, once said: 'Of all the many men and women who come to see me, over sixty per cent are suffering from no definable neurosis, but from a sense of the emptiness and senselessness and purposelessness of their lives. They nearly all need someone to love them and to trust them, and to show God to them.'

St. Augustine knew the answer: 'Our hearts are restless till they rest in Thee.' We cannot face life without fear, or even enjoy its happiness to the full unless we know that whatever happens we cannot drift beyond His love and care. *The basis of an unshakable stability is to know that we are loved individually by God. And this is the assurance that the Bible gives us.* It is the thread which holds it all together. It is the one experience tested and proved amid every kind of circumstance, of which the men who fill its pages were all sure. Whatever else in life is uncertain, this is sure, and on it we can build our lives. To trust the unchanging love of God is the secret of security that becomes surer with every act of trust. Like a strong foundation it becomes more real and solid with every stone we lay upon it.

But this security is consistent with freedom and all its risks. We sometimes ask how One who loves us so can permit us to suffer, to meet with danger and risk and sudden death. In their best moments the saints have always known that there is here no contradiction. 'God is our refuge and strength; therefore will we not fear, though the earth be moved.' They had no illusion about life and its power to hurt. They saw around them a world where it was possible that the hills might move; the most stable things might pass. Yet God remained their refuge. This very risk and uncertainty has always been God's method of education. 'As an eagle stirreth up her nest and scattereth her young . . .'—to teach them to use their wings—'so the Lord did lead them.' *A world without risk of mistake would be one where man would not grow.* Without pain or tears there would be no possibility of learning sympathy and tenderness, for we know men as hard as nails because they had everything their own way become soft and tender through the suffering of some beloved child. Many a youth coddled in comfort has come to thank God for the misfortune that flung him out to find his fate and develop his manhood. Even if God gave us a foolproof, painfree world, the first thing we should do with it would be to pull it down about our ears. There is a purpose in the risk and in the danger. Beneath and in it all God's love and care abide.

How can we know this? The secret is in Jesus. His love is the one permanent thing in a changing world. They tried to destroy that love, to put it out by insult and death. But through all that men could do His love shone undimmed, becoming the brighter through the very blows that sought to bludgeon it out of existence. If we look, we can find our comfort there.

Further reading:

The Problem of Pain (C. S. Lewis, Fontana).

Discuss:

1. 'Our hearts are restless till they rest in Thee.'
2. What is security?
3. Why does God allow suffering?

HAS CHRISTIANITY FAILED?

In one form or another this question is often asked: *'Since this world is in such chaos and misery after nearly two thousand years of Christianity, surely it seems that Christianity has failed?'*

The truthful answer to that question is both 'Yes' and 'No.' If the questioner means, 'Has Christianity failed to convert the whole world?' then the answer is obviously 'Yes.' In this country, for example, it is doubtful whether more than three per cent can be described as Christians in the New Testament sense of the term. If, on the other hand, the questioner means, 'Has Christianity failed to do any part of what it originally set out to do?' then the answer is just as obviously 'No.' The undisputed fact is that while Christianity has not secured universal approval, it has maintained the standards of its Founder and achieved an enormous amount.

The mistake in the critic's mind who thinks that Christianity has failed completely, is the critic's assumption that *if Christianity is true, then it must be assured of an immediate and complete success.* This is a false assumption: a mistake which some make when they say that if only the clergy would preach the Gospel properly they would fill their churches. Such critics overlook the fact that *the one Person who beyond dispute preached the full and unadulterated Gospel was crucified for doing so, and had but eleven adherents to show for a life's work.* The unattractive fact is that we have no guarantee that the truth of Jesus Christ's religion will ever be popular at all. The possibility that Christianity will ever become universally acceptable is left an open question in the New Testament writings. There is a strong case to be made out that *Christianity is likely to remain a minority movement,* and if this is so, then, so far as counting heads is concerned, it will always be a failure, as it has been from the beginning.

On the other hand, Christianity in every generation, including our own, has produced, *and is producing,* its minority quota of saints, martyrs and missionaries, who are vessels of God's grace and lights of the world in their several generations. Christianity makes its most important goal the attainment of character. It teaches that to believe in Jesus Christ means to obey Him, and to make a sincere attempt to be as much like Him as possible. In producing this kind of holiness, the Christian faith has succeeded.

We look again at the question, 'Has Christianity failed?' To be the popular religion of the masses—yes, so far it has. It continues to be rejected by millions. But that is no valid criticism of Christianity, any more than the action of Judas is a just criticism of Jesus Christ.

But has Christianity ever failed to produce the Lord's minority —the little leaven which the whole lump could be leavened by if it wished? The answer to that is an emphatic 'No.'

All through history a tiny Christian minority has had to stand firm, alone, amid an indifferent majority; in order to uphold the mind of Jesus Christ. Earlier it was over such things as slavery and the care of the sick, the aged and the helpless. In more recent times it has been over such things as marriage and divorce and the colour bar. Christianity took possession of the ancient world, not only as the religion of love, but also as the religion of truth. *So long as the Christian Church faithfully proclaims the character of Jesus Christ as the standard of what human conduct ought to be, it cannot be said to have failed.* It can only fail if it lowers this standard, so that people think they can follow Jesus Christ on their own terms.

That would be failure indeed.

Further reading:

Any good history of the Christian Church, as recommended by the parish priest.

Modern missionary literature.

The Early Church in Eastern England and *The Early Church in Eastern Northumbria* (Margaret Gallyon, Terence Dalton Ltd., Lavenham, Suffolk).

The Church: Its Changing Image through Twenty Centuries (Eric Jay, S.P.C.K.).

Discuss:

1. What is our estimate of 'successful living'?
2. Will Christians always be in a minority?
3. Standards—relative and absolute.
4. 'The History of the Church is a cordial for drooping spirits.'

ASKING THE RIGHT QUESTIONS ABOUT CHRIST

Those of us who do jigsaw puzzles or attempt the more difficult crosswords have often found that one particular piece or word opens the way to completing the puzzle or crossword; and until we find this piece or word we are held up. Something like this is also true in religious matters. When you are faced with a particular religious problem, you often find that when you have found the answer to one particular question, you have found the answer to many others. The difficulty is that sometimes we ask the wrong questions, and sometimes even if we ask the right questions we often get the wrong answers.

This is particularly true of the resurrection of Jesus. Many of us, when we are faced with the words in the Creed: 'and the third day he rose again from the dead,' tend to ask such questions as 'What really happened on the first Easter Day? Did Jesus really show himself alive?' And in order to answer these questions, we study the Bible and find that the stories are perplexing and do not give us clear answers, partly because they are written from different standpoints and emphasize different aspects.

The fact of the matter is that when we ask such questions we are asking the wrong questions first. We can only ask and try to answer such questions when we have first answered a much more fundamental one: *'Who was this person who is said to have risen again and shown Himself alive after death to His friends?'* Upon our answer to this question will depend the answers to these other questions.

Who, then, was Jesus? Let us suppose we say, 'Jesus was a remarkable human being who lived in the first century, and was a gifted healer and preacher, and was put to death as a criminal by His enemies.' Now this is a true statement as far as it goes. But it only goes so far as to rank Jesus among other remarkable human beings of whom there have been many in different spheres of life and achievement. If this is *all* we can say about Jesus, then we shall naturally go on to say that the resurrection is just a pious story put out by His friends, and that the tomb was not really empty on the first Easter Day. It could not have been, because no one has ever heard of a human being, however remarkable, coming to life again. So it cannot have happened in Jesus' case. We have here asked the right question, but from the Christian point of view we have given the wrong answer, and the resurrection and the empty tomb are dismissed as meaningless.

Who, then, was Jesus? Let us suppose we say (as Christians have always said) He was more than a remarkable human being, and add that He was also, in a very real sense, *God in human form on earth.*

To say this is to say that such a tremendous *miracle* has occurred that all other miracles, including the resurrection, pale into insignificance beside it. This is how an ancient writer put it many years ago: 'He who so loved the world that for our sakes He was made in time, through whom all times were made; was made man who made man; was created of a mother whom He created; was carried by hands which He formed; cried in the manger in wordless infancy; He, the word without whom all human eloquence is muted.'

The fact is that if we really believe that God came down to earth at Christmas, then the resurrection and the empty tomb seem thoroughly appropriate and suitable. As Peter said, in a sermon in Acts, 'God raised him to life again, set him free from the pangs of death because it could not be that death should keep him in its grip' (Acts 2: 24).

It is only when we start saying the *right* things about Jesus that

Easter Day begins to make sense. That is the reason why Jesus showed Himself alive after Good Friday only to those who had already begun to ask the right questions about Him, and give the right answers. He did not show Himself to Pontius Pilate or Herod or Caiaphas or other unbelievers. There was not much point because they had not even started to ask the right questions, much less give the right answers.

Further reading:

Miracles (C. S. Lewis, Collins or Fontana Books).

Discuss:

1. Who was Jesus?
2. 'If Christ's claims are untrue, they are those of a madman.
3. 'Before Abraham was, I am.'
4. How ought our attitude to this life to be influenced by the knowledge that the Son of God was truly Man?

ARE YOU A CHRISTIAN?

It is easy to answer the question, 'Are you a Christian?' If you have been baptized in the name of the Father, and of the Son, and of the Holy Ghost, as Jesus said in St. Matthew 28 : 19, then you are a Christian; if not, then you are not. But it is not so easy to answer the question, 'Are you a *good* Christian?' One's Christian life and witness is something like the mercury in a barometer —sometimes it stands high, and sometimes low, according to surrounding conditions. It is something like this with our faith and trust in God and our devotion to our Lord Jesus Christ. It has an up and down tendency; sometimes it stands higher, sometimes lower.

It varies considerably even from day to day, though this must not be exaggerated. But over a long period, say a year or a number of years, there is in every one an overall persistent falling away or an overall persistent rising up in the Christian faith and the Christian life. Nobody over a long term is static, staying on the same unshifting level of the Christian life year after year, with no increase or degeneration. We used to be taught that nature abhors a vacuum. In the same way, the Christian life abhors a static level and it just does not happen.

The falling-away process is too well known to need much comment, and it begins amongst the very youngest members of the Christian community. Even now, in present day England, if every new Sunday School child remained faithful, then every church in this country would be crammed to capacity every Sunday. But it does not happen, because at every age some drop off until the old Christians are comparatively few. The number of really Christian funerals that a priest takes, for example, are few indeed.

Now, this falling-off in the Christian life is nothing new. Our Lord had a good deal to say about what to expect when the Christian life was found to be hard going. St. Paul complained to the Corinthians and again to the Galatians over precisely the same things, and St. John, in the Book of the Revelation when writing to the small Christian communities in Asia Minor, particularly in Laodicea, tells of lukewarmness, deadness, and a decreasing faith in those who were once glad and joyful converts. But on the other hand, one sees in a few Christian souls the other process at work —the building-up process. There is to be seen in a good number, if one knows where to look for it, increasing achievement in the Christian life. It is seen in the classical sense in many older and faithful Christians, and in many young ones, too, who are consciously placing their hands in the hand of God to lead them without reserve into some vocation or place of special service.

There is, then, this process of increasing or decreasing, and there cannot be one of us who in his heart of hearts does not want to make good in the Christian life and to be on the side of the saints. But making this come true is a long-term policy. Indeed, the art of Christian living is probably the longest term activity in which any man engages. *It takes a life-time of Christian living and devotion and worship to reproduce the character of Christ in some measure in any man.* That is why the principal characteristics of the Christian are endurance and fortitude and a great patience in Eucharistic worship and private devotion and other religious duties, and almsgiving and all good works. This happens to be the way in which Christian living operates.

In Knaresborough, in Yorkshire, there is a well which is constantly refilled with a small waterfall. The water has certain mineral properties, and in the well you will find all manner of things, like gloves and boots, which people have thrown in and left there. If you come back after a day or two, the object is not much changed, but if you come back after several months the object has become encrusted and calcified—petrified into a stone glove or boot, owing to the nature and property of the water. As the water drops down day by day the things in it partake of the nature of the water to which they are constantly exposed. But it takes a long time. It is like this with the Christian life. Attendance at one celebration of the Holy Communion, or just one occasional prayer offered when up against it, makes little difference. One is much the same afterwards as before. *But if one constantly presents oneself to the Blessed Sacrament; if one does not give up saying one's prayers because it is hard; if one constantly exposes oneself to these holy influences of our Lord, then one takes on imperceptibly, at least in part, the nature of the Lord Himself.* It could hardly be otherwise. Here is the great value of a well-considered and regularly revised Rule of Life.

One sometimes envies the person who has had some sudden religious experience and who, because of it, became a fairly good Christian fairly quickly. But for most of us this does not happen. Most of us were probably brought into contact with the Christian faith from early years, and have never had any sudden religious experience. We find all the slowness of the going in the Christian life and all the discouragements, but if we give Christ's Body, the Church, a real chance, then we also find and know the very great comfort and heart-warming that comes from belonging to this body, with all its discipline, experience and sacraments of grace, and with its cheerful good company of like-minded Christian triers.

Further reading:

Records of Christianity (Ayerst and Fisher, Blackwell).

Discuss:

1. What is conversion?
2. 'Let patience have her perfect work.'
3. Why do many drop off from Church-going and Church discipline?

CHAPTER II

Reading the Holy Bible

THE OLD TESTAMENT

Some Wrong Ideas

MANY people unfortunately have spoken of the Old Testament as though God personally dictated to the writers word for word what they were to put down; in fact, one might sometimes imagine that the whole Bible had been dropped down complete from Heaven. What we have to understand is that the Old Testament was written by very ordinary people who lived between two and three thousand years ago, people who had very limited knowledge, and many of them simple and imperfect ideas about God.

One very important thing to remember about the Old Testament is that it is the writings of a people who were being trained to understand God and to know Him, and that it was written by those people at different times, from the point of view of their idea of God when they wrote, and that they were not writing with any idea that what they wrote would form a sacred book. Part of the Old Testament is a history of these people, and there is no doubt that the early part of their history was not written down until years after, some of it centuries after the events happened.

The history begins with Abraham. That is the beginning of the Jewish people, the time from which they always date their beginning. Abraham was called to leave his own country and to separate himself from other people for a *purpose*—the purpose contained in the promise 'In thy seed shall all the nations of the earth be blessed.' The seed or, in other words, the descendant, meant Christ. That was the beginning of the training of one nation in order that one day Christ might come into the world. This is why they are called the Chosen Race, chosen for a *purpose,* not a privilege. Abraham is the first historical character mentioned, and anything which comes before his time was not written as history.

The Laws of Moses

One of the first parts of the Old Testament to be written down was the Ten Commandments by Moses. In the course of hundreds of years, all the many other laws which are found in the first books of the Old Testament were added, as different cases arose for judgment and decision. New laws were made, just as we make new laws to-day, and many of them are laws which applied only to the particular kind of life they were leading, and therefore made only to agree with their primitive ideas of justice. For example, these are two laws out of the Book of Exodus: 'If an ox gore a man or a woman that they die, then shall the ox be surely stoned and its flesh shall not be eaten.' 'Thou shalt not suffer a witch to live.' How primitive are the ideas which are expressed in these laws and how far removed we think them to-day from a proper understanding about God and His will! That was in their very early days when they had a great deal to learn about God.

Legends and Folk Tales

Handed down by word of mouth, and not written at first, were many old tales which were made up to explain things which they did not understand.

For instance, they knew that tradition said there had once been a great flood. It had covered all the land where they had once lived and they thought in those early days that where they lived was the whole world; that if one went far enough in any direction, one would come to the end of the world. There arose in the minds of many people the question 'How is it that there are still not only people but also many different kinds of animals if the whole world was flooded?' So there grew up the folk tale of Noah building the ark and saving two of every animal. We know better now and we do not need this explanation. We know that there was a flood in that part of the world; archaeologists tell us that this is true; but we also know it was only a small part of the world which was in fact flooded.

Another question which worried these primitive people was this. 'Why are there so many languages in the world?' So there grew up the tale of the Tower of Babel—how that men tried to build a tower to heaven and in order to stop them the gods caused each of the builders to speak a different language and so caused confusion which made it impossible for them to continue their work.

The same thing is true about the account of Adam and Eve in the Garden of Eden. Some thoughtful people asked if, when the world was made, everything was good and God did not make either sin or evil, where did they come from? There were other early tribes who also wanted an answer to this question, and the tale of Adam and Eve was one that was well known to them too. The Jews took this tale and put it in their book, but the wonderful thing is that they took out of it all its heathen coarseness and turned it into a tale with sublime thoughts, wonderfully simply expressed. It tells us quite simply that sin is disobedience, and that all the evils of the world come from man disobeying God. We know that this is true.

The Prophets

For many, the most helpful parts of the Old Testament are the Books of the Prophets; but even the Prophets themselves had to learn very gradually about God and His will. There is a great difference between the early Prophets and the later ones. For example, Samuel could tell the people to do dreadful things, and say that God wished them to be done. He told Saul to go to punish the Amalekites for having stopped the Israelites from passing through their land four hundred years before. Samuel thought that this was what God wanted and, in addition, that not only should the Amalekites be defeated, but that every living thing in their land should be put to death.

How different is all this from the teaching of the later Prophets, who had gradually learned more and more about God and who could write such things as: 'What does the law require of thee but to do justly and to love mercy and to walk humbly with thy God,' or 'Let judgment roll down as waters and righteousness as a mighty stream,' or the last of the Prophets, who had such a deep understanding about God that he could write 'He was despised and rejected of man, a Man of sorrows and acquainted with grief. Surely he hath borne our griefs and carried our sorrows. He was wounded for our transgressions and with his stripes we are healed. All we like sheep have gone astray, we have turned every one to his own way and the Lord hath laid on him the iniquity of us all.'

How very different all this is from the earlier parts of the Old Testament! During the long course of their history the Jewish people are at last approaching the day when Jesus can be born on earth. The Old Testament is meant to show us how, gradually, a very primitive people is trained to have lofty and noble ideas of God, until they are ready for all that happens in the New Testament.

If the question is asked, 'Is the Old Testament true?' the answer is that it is the true writings of the Jewish people during their long history when they were being gradually trained to understand and to know God, but they are also writings where historical facts are mixed up with primitive tales and legends, each part written sincerely and truthfully as far as they understood truth, until at last, through the Holy Ghost (who 'spake by the Prophets,' as we say in the Nicene Creed), they arrived at a deep understanding of God. Now they are ready for that day to which all their training has led them—'the fulness of time when God could send forth his Son born of a woman, born under the law.'

THE NEW TESTAMENT

Were they Real People?

Our starting point is that nineteen hundred years ago Jesus Christ went about preaching and teaching up and down Galilee and Judæa, and that after a ministry of three years, His enemies secured His condemnation before the Roman governor, Pontius Pilate, and had Him put to death by crucifixion. It is interesting to notice what heathen historians were saying at the same time, and we have all this vouched for outside the New Testament by historians living at the same time, who were not the slightest bit interested in Jesus. The famous Roman historian, Tacitus, writes, 'Christ, from whom the Christians receive their name, had, during the Emperorship of Tiberius, been taken and punished by Pontius Pilate.'

The Gospel is Spread

During His ministry our Lord gathered around Him a band of loyal men, disciples, who were willing to learn and who came to recognize, even during His lifetime, that He was no ordinary preacher and teacher but was, as they said, 'the Christ, the Son of the living God.' Being convinced, in a way that left no room for doubt, that after His crucifixion He had been raised by God from the dead, these disciples, and others who joined their fellowship, began to tell others about Him 'in Jerusalem and in all Judæa and in Samaria and unto the uttermost part of the earth' (Acts 1 : 8). They announced that Jesus was the Messiah by whom God would save men and would establish His Kingdom.

The Great Apostle, Saint Paul

The New Testament gives a tremendous place to one among these early followers, an enthusiastic young Jew, Saul (or Paul) of Tarsus, who was at first a bitter enemy and persecuted all the followers of Jesus. But he was strangely converted and after that worked very hard to carry the good news about Jesus throughout the length and breadth of the then known world. Most people who know what he did would include St. Paul among the ten greatest men in the history of the world. If you want to know the story you will find accurate evidence, first in those remarkable letters which he himself wrote, and, secondly, in the Book of the Acts written by his doctor and travel companion, St. Luke. The letters of St. Paul, of which we have only a few, were mostly written within twenty to thirty years after Jesus was put to death —that is to say, *before* the Gospels which, in our New Testament, they follow.

Reliable Authors

It is important also to understand that the books of the New Testament were written by people who had a good knowledge of the things of which they wrote. Famous scholars agree that the Acts is a most carefully composed and trustworthy piece of writing. Sir William Ramsey, one of the foremost of writers of ancient history, has said that its author (St. Luke) is to be placed 'among the historians of the first rank.' An interesting fact is that in various parts of his narrative (for instance in Chapter 27, the story of the voyage to Rome) St. Luke uses the *first* personal pronoun—*we* sailed, *we* came—showing that he himself was present on those occasions. These parts of the Book of the Acts are probably taken from his personal diary. St. Paul needed a doctor with him because he suffered from what he calls 'a thorn in the flesh.' This was an illness, probably recurring fits of epilepsy, or a form of blindness.

Similarly, we have good reason to trust the accounts of our Lord's public teaching given in the Gospels. The earliest of the four Gospels was that of Mark and it was written about A.D. 65. It was, incidentally, dictated by Peter, who was not a scholar, to the young Mark, who was the young man who fled from our Lord when He was arrested, leaving his cloak in the hands of one of the soldiers. This is related in St. Mark 14: 51 and 52. St. Mark's Gospel is, therefore, really that of St. Peter.

St. Matthew's Gospel was written by a man who was writing to convert to Christianity the Jewish people, so he quotes a great deal from the Prophets who foreshadowed the coming of Christ.

St. Luke was an educated Greek and his Gospel was written to convert the Greek speaking people. If you look at the first few verses of St. Luke's Gospel and the first few verses of the Acts of the Apostles (which is his second volume) you will find that both books are dedicated to the same man—a certain Theophilus—who helped St. Luke to publish his writings. St. Luke's Gospel has been called 'the most beautiful book in the world.'

The latest of the Gospels was that of St. John, and this was written some time after A.D. 90. It sets the Crown on all that the other writers have taught, and expands most wonderfully what the other Evangelists have written, because the writer seems to have entered much more deeply into the mind of the Master. He is thought to be the only one of the Twelve to escape martyrdom.

Why the Gospels were Written

The Gospels are all reminiscences of people who had known Jesus while He was on earth, and had heard Him preach His unforgettable parables, and had seen His tender sympathy with those who were suffering, or in need, His forgiving attitude towards His accusers, His unflinching courage in the face of opposition, danger and death. These people tell what they remember about Him, for the simple reason that, like St. Peter before the Sanhedrin (the Jewish Council), they 'cannot but speak of the things which they have seen and heard.'

All this makes it plain that the New Testament writings are in a very different class from the legendary stories which have grown up around the name of Buddha and other religious teachers of the ancient world. It does not follow, however, that everything in the New Testament is to be accepted as accurate history. It is as well, in this connection, to remind ourselves how the four Gospels came to be written. While the authors never wrote down anything but what they believed to be true, their aim in writing certainly was not to provide readers in the twentieth century with a detailed and accurate history book about our Lord and His followers. If that had been their aim, we may be sure that they would have included much that has been left out, and made clear much that is still uncertain. The fact is that they wrote as men who had come to believe in Jesus. In the Gospels they have told, without pretending that it is a complete record, various stories and sayings which might help other people to see in Him 'the Christ, the Son of God' (St. John 20: 30 and 31).

This being the case, we cannot rule out altogether the possibility that sometimes what they believed may have affected what they wrote. But when all allowance has been made in such like cases for the possibility of misunderstanding, it remains true that the New Testament, taken as a whole, is a thoroughly reliable account of events which really happened.

Religious Truth

There is an important point to be kept in mind when we consider New Testament truths. A thing may not be literally true, and yet be true in a deeper and far more important sense. This is especially the case where religious truth is concerned. Many of the strange pictures in the Book of Revelation, for instance, are an attempt to show the war that is always going on between good and evil or, as we may say, between God and the devil. Some of the details in the picture, like the tales of the Beast which men are forced to worship, refer especially to the persecution of Christians under the Roman Emperor, and such things have happened in modern Europe. So too when we read in other parts of the New Testament of Heaven as a place of blessedness, apparently above the sky, and of hell as a place of torment with fire, we must understand that here are attempts to describe religious truth by word-pictures. It is stupid to interpret them as if they were literal facts.

Miracles

Do not for one moment doubt that our Lord did work miracles, or 'works of power,' as they are called in the Gospels. Jesus was filled with such a strong faith in God the Father that He was ready and able when necessary to show His faith in action. It was these wonderful acts of divinity which so aroused the anger of the Pharisees. 'The whole world has gone after him' they said. In all the Gospels, *first place* is given to our Lord's miracles.

What the New Testament Tells Us

Whatever difficulties you may have about some of it, remember that the New Testament, from first to last, bears witness that Jesus was no ordinary prophet, but was God revealed in human form, one who, in His human life, showed the holiness and love and power which we think of when we think of God Himself. It is this fact, combined with the stories of His miraculous Birth and Resurrection, which have made Christians of all ages believe that He is alive for evermore, and is the Conqueror over sin and death. The New Testament can never be understood so long as a man is content to think of our Lord as merely one of the world's great heroes, but once he sees in Him that God has done something unique for the world, sending, as we say, His own Son to accomplish the world's salvation, then the New Testament will become the most wonderful book in the world; all the more wonderful because he knows it to be true; and he will read it regularly until he knows its contents by heart.

Further reading:

Any modern translations of the Bible.
Any volumes of the *Clarendon Bible,* or Moffatt's *New Testament Commentary.*
Commentary on the New Testament (E. M. Blaiklock, Hodder & Stoughton).
Theology and the Gospel of Christ (E. L. Mascall, SPCK).
The Dead Sea Scrolls (Geza Vermes, Collins).
Reading the New Testament today (Beck, Lutterworth Press).
The Bible (John Muddiman).

Beginning of Old Testament Study (ed. John Rogerson, SPCK).
The Old Testament and the Archaeologist (H. Darrell Lane, SPCK).
The Letters of Paul (C. J. Roetzel, SCM Press).

Discuss:

1. If the Bible had not been written, is there any other imaginable quarter from which we could have had that which it contains?
2. The Bible believes in God, and the Bible believes in man.
3. The purpose of God is bound up with the salvation of man.
4. Ought we to be opposed to 'criticism' of the Bible?
5. How far is it possible to use the Bible as a guide to the choice of road, an illumination to the work of our hands, and an inspiration to the thoughts of our minds?

CHAPTER III

What is the Church?

THIS question, though simple in terms, is far from simple in fact; and not only can many answers be given to it, but these answers are bound up with endless controversy. It is wise to confine our attention to certain main aspects of the subject which concern all types of churchmen, even though different schools would express them differently or would add much to what will be said.

Let us look at four things about the Church—*First:* its origin; *second:* its structure; *third:* its allegiance; and *fourth:* its mission.

(1) Obviously the Church is a form of association. It is the organized association of people who profess to believe and follow Jesus Christ, but it does not take its origin as ordinary associations —political, industrial, social—do. These are formed of people of similar views or interests joining together in a society or club or federation. What then is it, more than this? We must get hold of this at the outset, even though it be a high plane from which to begin. The point may be put thus: The Church is *not,* in essence and origin, an organization or association, but what is described as an *organism.*

What is an organism, as distinct from an organization or association? We see the answer to this if we look at the nature of the being of man. We might look at a man externally and say that he is an association of flesh, bone, blood and so on, but we all know that this collocation is not what is a man. He is a living whole, in which all these elements are united into one being. So is it with the Church. It is not merely an association of people holding common religious opinions and co-operating for common religious ends. *It is an organic whole, the originating, vitalizing and unifying fact in which is Christ.* Indeed, the New Testament describes the Church by this very figure—the body of Christ; and here is quite a different idea from merely a fortuitous association of people forming a Christian club.

Now, this to some may seem mystical and unreal, but it is no more so than is the spiritual life of the individual Christian. The individual is a Christian man because Christ is his life, and this society is the Christian Church in the same way. In both, the creative fact is Christ—He is in the personal life of the individual Christian, and is also common to the associated lives of all Christians. Thus, a man united to Christ is by that fact united to all Christians. As one of the early fathers says: 'Where Jesus Christ is, there is the Catholic Church.' This is the spiritual fact which is the foundation of the Church and differentiates it from all human associations. It is spiritual, which means not that it is unreal, for spiritual fact is as real as material, but that it is not apparent to the outward senses, just as the soul of man is not.

(2) Let us still think of the nature of man. We have seen that a collection of various elements does not make a man, but that the unifying and vitalizing principle within (what we call the spirit or the soul) does that. On the other hand, the spirit or soul without the body is not man, and would be but a ghost. So, again, it is with Christ and His Church. He is the vital principle, but that needs an external form for its life and work in the world—hence the Church's structure, its organization, which is called the visible Church. Perhaps that expression is unfortunate, because people easily think that there are two churches—one visible and one invisible. There is, and there can be, one Church, because there is but one Christ who alone originates the Church. The visible Church is not another Church, but the spiritual reality of the Church made visible in a corporate form for its life in this world.

It is just here that complications and errors and divisions arise. In the first place, in thus becoming visible, the Church becomes mixed and imperfect, because what is outward may be falsely assumed. *The inward reality of the Church cannot be counterfeited, but anything of its structure can—creed, profession, or ritual ceremony or official status.* As history so clearly and painfully shows, there are many in the soul of the Church who are not of its body, and very many who are of its body who are not of its soul. *Yet the Church must have its body in this world, and this inevitable imperfection in its outward expression is reason. not for holding aloof from the visible Church, but rather for our continually seeking its purification through the spirit of its Creator.*

Again, when the Church thus takes an outward form, the outward things of its structure easily come to be regarded as the creative things of its life. It is one thing (and a right thing) to say that the Church on earth must have a visible ecclesiastical system. It is quite another thing (and a wrong thing) to say that this ecclesiastical system—be it Episcopalian, or Presbyterian, or any other—is what makes the Church. Confusion about this is prevalent in many minds. To avoid it, let us keep clear the distinction between what the Church *is* and what it *has*. The Church, as we have seen, *is* a spiritual organism—Christ living in His people and uniting them to one another in Himself. It *has* ecclesiastical organization; and while the more perfectly it has this, the better; still, even where it has it imperfectly, that is a defect in the expression of the Church's life, rather than the destruction of the life itself. *While we do well to value what is called the ecclesiastical order, we must not let our theory of this outstrip what the action of the Holy Spirit (who is Christ living and acting) countenances and corroborates;* if our ecclesiastical systems were always made subject to this test, then many of the things which divide churches would be kept in their proper place.

(3) One reason for these differences about matters in the ecclesiastical structure is that Christ has not prescribed that structure, but has left His Church to organize itself, and many have differed as to how to carry out His mind and will in matters of government and the like; but *on one point Christ was quite explicit—He alone is the Church's Head.* In all spiritual matters, such as faith, worship, discipline and morals, the Church must be free from any secular control from the State or elsewhere, in order to listen to and learn and follow His voice alone, as it is revealed in His word and by His spirit. This is what is called the spiritual freedom of the Church, and the way to understand it is to realize that it is simply the Church claiming, exactly as the Christian man claims, to have a conscience. The faithful Christian man will not allow the State or any other secular authority to rule him in matters of religion, and neither will the faithful Church. Both recognize the right of the State to rule in things which are not of conscience—in, for example, property; but *in matters of religious faith and practice, the Christian man observes only his Christian conscience, and so also does the Church.* This is the only genuine

'high' churchism; which is not a matter of clericalism, still less of ritualism. In that the Church is Christ's and in all spiritual things must be free to obey its one Head. *A Church which is not (and which is not ready, if necessary, to suffer that it may be), a system of conscience towards Christ, has lost the very idea of what the Church is by losing the idea of whose it is.*

(4) Only a word needs to be added on the Church's mission, and it leads us to the further question not merely of what the Church is, but what it is for.

The Church does not exist for its own sake or to conserve its own interests. *Its ends are three: As regards God, to glorify His Name and do His will; as regards its own members, to train them in Christian faith and character; and as regards the world, to proclaim the love and law of Christ in the Gospel, and thus to convert more to Him and to serve His kingdom.* How far it comes short in the attainment of these ends, we can all see; but so does each one of us, who calls himself a Christian, come short. So, therefore, we ought not on this ground to rail at the Church's failings, nor to give up our loyalty to it. We should rather rally to it and devote ourselves to its service.

I. THE HOLY CATHOLIC CHURCH

The idea is still often held that it is possible to be a good Christian without having any contact with the Church. This means that people think that to believe in the Church and all that it demands of a man is outside the scope of simple Christianity—which is supposed to consist only in personal honesty and active goodness, linked up, perhaps, with some general belief in God.

This idea, however, is certainly not supported by the New Testament. Certainly the duties of personal goodness are stressed by the writers as being among the duties of a disciple of Christ, but the 'Christian' was also a 'member of the Christian Church,' and a *good* Christian is a worshipping, working, witnessing member of the Christian Church. This is shown in several passages in the Acts of the Apostles in which those who wished to become Christians were shown that the way was to become, through Baptism, members of the Christian Church. (You might look up Acts 2: 38; 8: 38; 9: 18.)

To cultivate and show qualities which are proper to followers of

Christ does not in itself *make any one a Christian. He is not a Christian unless he is a member of the Christian Church, for Christ's religion is a fellowship.* The question may be asked why this is so and why a man cannot be a Christian 'on his own.' In reply it may be said that from the very first the people of God were formed into a Church; and that the Christian Church is, so to speak, founded upon the Jewish Church which had existed for centuries before our Lord came to earth. It is also true to say that great ideals cannot be, as it were, left to take their chance in the world. There must be a body of people whose duty it will be to see that they are spread and taught. But however this may be, in fact our Lord did say: 'I will build My Church'; and appointed Baptism as the rite of admittance into the Church, and Holy Communion as the sacred meal of the members of His Body. Moreover, it is most inspiring to feel that we are not left to ourselves, nor do we even belong to a little group of like-minded people in one particular place, but our membership is to a world-wide society which 'thinks in continents' and must not rest until the sign of Christ, His Holy Cross, is planted in the soul of every nation.

II. THE ANGLICAN COMMUNION

This phrase, 'The Anglican Communion,' is usually employed when we refer to any of the dioceses which are in full communion with the see of Canterbury. It is worth noting, however, that in recent years there are other Churches—for example, the Old Catholics—with which, happily, Anglicans have come into full communion, though they are not regarded as parts of the Anglican Communion.

At the end of the sixteenth century there were in England and Ireland less than 50 Anglican bishops, but the recent growth of the Anglican Communion—mainly in the last 200 years—has been remarkable. (It is interesting to observe that not much more than 100 years ago Australia formed part of the Archdeaconry of Calcutta.) In 1867, when the first Lambeth Conference was held, there were 144 Anglican bishops entitled to an invitation to Lambeth, although only 76 were able and willing to attend. In 1930 nearly 400 bishops were entitled to an invitation, and the number today, when Suffragans are included, considerably larger.

What is the Lambeth Conference?

The Lambeth Conference is the name given to the periodical assemblies of bishops of the Anglican Communion which, since 1867, have met at Lambeth Palace, the London home of the Archbishop of Canterbury. The Lambeth Conference normally takes place every ten years.

Their Origin

The idea of these meetings of our bishops was first suggested in a letter to the Archbishop of Canterbury by Bishop Hopkins of Vermount in 1851, but nothing was done. Then, eleven years later, the bishops of the Church in Canada, who were perplexed by various problems, requested the Archbishop (Dr. Longley) to call 'a national Synod of the bishops of the Anglican Church at home and abroad.' The Archbishop, after consultation with both houses of the Convocation of Canterbury, assented, and the first Lambeth Conference took place in 1867. There were some in those days who regarded such a Conference with grave misgivings. The Archbishop of York and certain other bishops declined to attend, and Dean Stanley refused the use of Westminster Abbey for the closing service of the Conference. This seems very strange to us, but we must remember that the Church was troubled then by the alleged heresy of Bishop Colenso, and it was supposed by some that this first Lambeth Conference would prove to be the initiation of a determined heresy hunt. In his opening address, however, Dr. Longley made it clear that the bishops were meeting 'to discuss matters of practical interest' and, in fact, the Lambeth Conference has never sought to adjudicate on matters of domestic theological controversy. *Its resolutions have naturally great moral weight, though they are not to be regarded as binding on the consciences of all Churchpeople.* On the whole, however, they have been characterized by great wisdom and charity.

Successive Lambeth Conferences have been true to the genius of our English Church, which seeks always to lead rather than to coerce. Any fair-minded person reading the reports of these Conferences will feel that here are the conclusions of men mindful of their apostolic office and who wait upon the guidance of the Holy Spirit.

Achievements

Each Lambeth Conference reminds us of the splendid achievements under God of our English part of the Catholic and Apostolic Church. A hundred and twenty years ago, there were few bishops of our Anglican Church in other lands. In 1841, Bishop Blomfield of London founded the Colonial Bishoprics Fund. Less than 50 years later it had collected and expended a sum of £840,000 for 55 new bishoprics overseas. Each bishop comes to the Conference as the representative of thousands of Christian men and women who long for the rule on earth of our Lord Jesus Christ.

The Lambeth Conference is not 'just another of those meetings,' but a striking testimony to the power of God in the world to-day. From this little island there has grown a world-wide communion of Christian people, united in a common love of our Lord, a common possession of the apostolic ministry, a common use of the Creeds and Sacraments, a common love of the Bible, and a common life in Christ's Body, the Church. One of the factors that, under God, has served to unite us, is our English Prayer Book which is used, with slight adaptations, in all parts of the Anglican Communion. This thought might well be in our minds sometimes when we meet together in God's House. The beautiful and moving prayers in our ordered worship are hallowed, not only by the thousands of those who have loved them and used them before us, but by the multitudes also of those who in other lands join with us in the same words of contrition, dedication and praise.

We can humbly rejoice before God that the abundance of spiritual life in our Anglican Communion, together with her traditional faith and order, bear witness to her part in the fuller life of the One, Holy, Catholic and Apostolic Church.

III. THE CHURCH OF ENGLAND

'The Church of England' is a term used to describe the two Provinces of Canterbury and York. At present, the Province of Canterbury contains 29 dioceses and the Province of York 14 dioceses.

It is important to emphasize that the true unit of Church life is not the parish but the diocese. We do *not* take a number of parishes and group them together in order to make a diocese. Instead, it may be said that we take the diocese—a local unit of Church Life under a Diocesan Bishop who is in charge of the Church throughout the area—and, divide it, for convenience and efficiency, into a number of parishes which are in the charge of various priests to whom the bishop 'parcels out' authority when they are put in charge of the living. This being so, any diocesan enterprise is the concern of all the people in the respective parishes.

It is a common mistake to suppose that the Church of England was formed only at the time of the Reformation. This is a complete error.

In the history of the Christian Church there have been two major breaks. First, in the year A.D. 1054, for the settlement of a dispute between the Churches, Pope Leo IX sent his legates to Constantinople, who later laid a degree of excommunication on the altar of the Church of St. Sophia—and the Eastern patriarchs were not slow in returning this compliment. So the division took place between what are loosely termed the Church of the East and the Church of the West. This is usually known as 'The Great Schism.'

Later on, in the sixteenth century, another division took place. There is not much point in recounting the details of the struggle. So far as our own country is concerned the Church and people in the reign of Henry VIII set aside the jurisdiction of the Bishop of Rome in this country. They did not deny his position and they did not withdraw themselves from him. The rest followed through the action of the Pope himself. Some years passed before Rome took action against the English Church and people; but on 27 April 1570, Pope Pius V issued a Bull of Excommunication against Queen Elizabeth; and the division between Canterbury and Rome was complete. All the complicated history of the struggle between Henry VIII and the Bishop of Rome can be read in the history books. This division is usually known as 'The Breach with Rome.'

It is quite clear that no new Church was founded in England at this time, as has sometimes been stated. For example, in the section of the Prayer Book which is entitled 'Concerning the service of the Church' (originally written by Archbishop Cranmer as a preface to the Prayer Book of 1549), reference is made to 'the service in this Church of England *these many years.*' In the thirtieth canon of 1603 it is said 'Far was it from the purpose of the Church of England to forsake and reject the Churches of Italy, France, Spain, Germany or any such like Church.' 'Ecclesia Anglicana' is referred to in Magna Charta. In many dioceses, which were created in Saxon and Norman times, there has been since that time a continuous succession of bishops until the present day. These dioceses were, of course, founded long before the time of the Reformation. The Archbishop of Canterbury has said that a member of the Church of England finds 'a system of Church Order which goes back in unbroken succession to the days of the Apostles.' It is most important to kill this persistent mistake of supposing that the Church of England dates from the reign of Queen Elizabeth. *The Church to which we belong is the Church which goes back in unbroken succession to the Church of the Apostles founded by our Lord Jesus Christ.*

IV. ANGLICAN PRINCIPLES

At one of the Lambeth Conferences, our bishops published four simple basic conditions upon which the Anglican Church bases her doctrine, and also upon which we in the Anglican Church are prepared to join up and reunite with any other Christians in the world. The four points are these:

(1) *The Scriptures.* The Holy Bible, Old and New Testaments, contains all that is necessary for salvation in Jesus Christ, and the Bible is the rule and standard of our faith. This means that any teaching or practice which cannot honestly and clearly be traced back to the Bible is not an essential part of Christianity. The Church rejects non-Scriptural beliefs, whether old or new.

(2) *The Creeds.* The Apostles' Creed, which we use, for example, at Mattins and Evensong, together with the Nicene Creed, which we use at the Holy Communion Service, are a full and sufficient statement of the Christian faith. In court, a witness has to tell the truth—that is, the facts; the whole truth—that is, no

omissions; and nothing but the truth—that is, no additions. Many people would very much like to omit some of the awkward and uncomfortable bits of the Christian faith. Others would like to add non-essential bits on to it. But these two creeds, together constitute for us the bare essentials of Christianity—the truth, the whole truth and nothing but the truth.

(3) *The Sacraments.* The two sacraments which were ordained by Christ Himself are Baptism (Christening) and the Holy Communion. Both are to be done with His own words, and using the elements which He used—water for Baptism, and bread and wine for the Holy Communion. In the New Testament there was only one way to join the Church, and that was by offering oneself for Baptism. And there was only one kind of specifically Christian worship that Jesus commanded to be continued, and that was the Holy Communion.

(4) *The Ministry.* The historic episcopate—the unbroken succession of bishops—whereby bishops make bishops, priests and deacons, by laying on of hands and prayer—goes back certainly to the second century. This ministry traces its authority not to self-appointment, nor to choice by a congregation, but to *ordination,* through a succession of persons reaching back through the ages to our Lord. (See also pp. 58–9.)

These four, then, the Scriptures, the Creeds, the Sacraments, and the Ministry, we Anglicans believe to be essentials to any effectively organized Christianity, and to any operative and living Church, and on these terms we welcome all comers of any colour, class or race. For ourselves, we regard these four things as the minimum requirements upon which it is possible to have lasting unity amongst Christian people. It is further worth saying that Anglicans are ready and eager to have completely free and equal partnership, brotherhood and unity with any other Christians in the world who will accept these four basic principles. This is what the Church of England stands for. Any form of Christianity which had no principles and no shape would very soon die out altogether. So we say to all comers, on this basis let us all be fellow-Christians together.

Further reading:

I believe in Man (George Carey, Hodder & Stoughton).
Voices in the Wilderness (John Bowden, SCM).
The Faith Abroad (J. D. Davies, Blackwells).

Discuss:

1. All must hold themselves to blame for some share in the divisions of Christendom.
2. The Church is holy because through her the holiness of Jesus Christ is passed on to mankind.
3. Whenever a Christian body draws its members from only a limited type of men and women the mark of catholicity is lost.
4. The opposite of 'catholic' is 'sectarian.'
5. 'The sheet-anchor of orthodoxy lies in the Apostolic Succession.'

APPENDIX I

NECESSARY BELIEFS AND PIOUS OPINIONS

The sixth Article states: 'Holy Scripture containeth all things necessary to salvation . . . '; and it is important to be clear about some of the issues involved.

On 1 November 1950, the Pope proclaimed a new Roman Catholic doctrine, the dogma of the corporal assumption into Heaven of the Blessed Virgin Mary. The Feast of the Assumption of the Blessed Virgin Mary on 15 August is observed by both Eastern and Western Christendom. In the East, the Feast is called 'The falling asleep of the Blessed Virgin Mary.' In our own Anglican Communion, the Feast has authority in that it appears in the Calendar of the Scottish Church and in that of the provinces of South Africa. Observance of the Feast does not necessarily imply belief that our Lady's earthly body was taken up into Heaven at her death. Many have always believed that the body which bore the sinless Son of God could never see corruption. Others, while not denying that this may be so, have been content not to dogmatize upon the question, but to observe the Feast as marking the assured passing of our Lady's soul to Heaven. In other words, as in the Roman Church until 1950, belief in the bodily ascension of our Lady into Heaven is a 'pious opinion,' firmly held by some; which others, while not denying, have seen no necessity for affirming. They point out that there is no evidence for belief in the doctrine prior to the sixth century. The doctrine proclaimed in 1950 thus became an integral part of the Roman Catholic faith, binding upon all members of the Roman Communion as necessary to salvation. Our own Archbishops at the time repudiated the necessity of the dogma on behalf of the Church of England. They said, 'The Church of England renders honour and reverence to the Mother of our Lord Jesus Christ. But there is not the smallest evidence in the Scriptures or in the teaching of the early Church of belief in the doctrine of her bodily assumption. The Church of England refuses to regard as requisite for a saving faith any doctrines or opinions which are not plainly contained in the Scriptures.'

We must not, however, lose sight of the truth that *all* Catholics believe that our Lady is in Heaven interceding for us. Those within the Roman Church who had not, prior to the 1950 doctrine, accepted the belief that our Lady's body was taken up into Heaven at her death, nevertheless believed in her heavenly intercession. As a writer at the time said: 'The honour of the Queen of all the Saints is not enhanced by association with extravagant speculation about the earthly circumstances of her translation into glory. For the most prudent Virgin who heard the word of God, and kept it, is Queen of the truth to which the world's disciples must bear witness. And no devotion can yield her honour unless it is rooted and grounded in the truth.'

Promulgation by the Papacy of a doctrine having 'no sure warrant in Scripture' is nothing new. In 1854, Pope Pius IX formally proclaimed the doctrine of the Immaculate Conception of our Lady, asserting that she was born without stain of original sin. Previously, this doctrine had been supported by the Franciscans, but as strongly opposed by the Dominicans. The Roman Council of Trent in the sixteenth century is ambiguous in many of its formularies, but certainly appears to regard Holy Scripture and tradition as equally valuable sources of doctrine. It is here that the vital difference between Rome and the reformed religious communities lies. If we believe that the Holy Spirit guided the Church in the selection of the books which make up the Holy

Scriptures, it is reasonable to believe also that no vital part of the revelation of God in Christ was suffered to be lost.

It is true, however, that the practical effects of Papal pronouncements of the kind mentioned have been small. Before the definition of the Immaculate Conception in 1854, it was feared that such a definition would have disastrous consequences, but the decree was quietly accepted. In 1870, at the Vatican Council, the Pope declared himself to be the infallible head of the Church. For months before, there had been intense feeling between the supporters and opponents of the doctrine. It was seriously proposed at a Cabinet meeting presided over by Mr. Gladstone that the powers should intervene to break up the Council. Yet the practical consequences of the decree of Papal Infallibility have been of the slightest, and Roman Catholics are divided as to whether the Pope has ever made an infallible utterance, and if so, how often. Again, towards the end of the last century, the Pope issued a bull formally condemning Anglican Orders, asserting that we have no priesthood in the Anglican Church. On its publication, no large secession took place (as had been forecast), and the main practical effect of the condemnation has been to cause Anglicans to consider more carefully the veracity of Papal claims before submitting to them. The practical effect of the 1950 formulation of a sixth century legend as an article of the Roman faith was to cast into relief the genius of the Anglican Communion as the exponent of that full Catholic faith which has its roots in antiquity and in the Holy Scriptures. If we do not ourselves personally endorse the doctrine of the bodily assumption, it should cause us to show that nevertheless we yield to none in our love for the Mother of God.

CHAPTER IV

What is contained in the Prayer Book?

ANGLICANS are largely people of the 1662 Prayer Book; and current liturgical revision should certainly not deflect us from an examination of its treasures.

The title page of the Prayer Book runs as follows: 'The Book of Common Prayer and Administration of the Sacraments and other Rites and Ceremonies of the Church according to the Use of the Church of England; together with the Psalter or Psalms of David pointed as they are to be sung or said in Churches; and the Form and Manner of Making, Ordaining and Consecrating of Bishops, Priests and Deacons.' We look therefore at these sections in turn:

I. 'THE BOOK OF COMMON PRAYER'

'Common Prayer' meant the Divine Office in its revised and reformed shape, consisting of two daily services—Morning and Evening Prayer (or Mattins and Evensong). These two services were a great simplification from the many of the old Latin service books. In the old days 'the number and hardness of the rules called the Pie (a sort of directory of worship), and the manifold changings of the service, was the cause, that to turn the book only was so hard and intricate a matter, that many times there was more business to find out what should be read, than to read it when it was found out.'

To Mattins and Evensong must be added the Litany, which Thomas Cranmer, drawing on various ancient sources, issued in English in 1544. This superb piece of English is wonderful 'said,' quite splendid when well sung. It has figured since 1549 in the Prayer Book and since 1662 has been directed to be said 'after Morning Prayer' on Sundays, Wednesdays and Fridays.

The term 'Common Prayer' implies an intention of the Reformers to make the Divine Office in its Prayer Book form an integral and necessary part of the devotional life of the whole Christian body, both clergy and laity. *The Divine Office was no longer to be the business of a spiritual and cloistered élite:* it was to be an obligation incumbent upon all. With this object, in addition to the all-important change from Latin into English and the reduction of the number of services to two, the services were greatly simplified: the result being that in the Church of England we came to possess at once a popular choir-office and one suitable for private use.

The Reformers stressed the Ministry of the Word as not less important than the Ministry of the Sacraments; and the new arrangement had an immense value as a means of instruction. The Scriptural 'Word' included the Psalms, with which worshippers now became very familiar.

II. 'THE ADMINISTRATION OF THE SACRAMENTS'

In making our approach to God we are hampered by our entanglement in the world of sense and our involvement with its claims. But material things need not be a barrier to spiritual things. God made both worlds; and there is a correspondence between the visible and the invisible, the outward and the inward, which supplies the key to some of the most characteristic features of Christian worship. It is the explanation of what we call the 'symbol'—the use of visible signs to express spiritual truths.

But visible signs may do still more: they may also become the vehicle by which spiritual reality is actually given. So from 'symbol,' we pass to 'sacrament.' As Evelyn Underhill has written: 'Symbols represent and suggest, whilst sacraments work. Effective action is essential to them; and this action is not from God to man, but from man to God.'

This 'sacramental principle' is fundamental to Christian worship. The principle finds its supreme expression in the Incarnation of the Son of God, which is the basic fact of the Christian faith. God in Jesus Christ takes upon Himself our human nature—partly that He can reveal Himself to men in a way they can understand; partly that He may consecrate the whole range of human existence and show how even its hard necessities may be used to help build up a life of perfect union with God; partly that by linking man in a close relationship with Himself, He may give to them divine strength without which this union cannot be achieved. *So the Christian Sacraments are 'the extension of the Incarnation,' using the same idea of the use of material things for a spiritual purpose, and also deriving all their efficacy in this respect from Him who is 'the Word made flesh.'* In them we see how God 'in Christ' can use even such common things as water and bread and wine to work upon the soul of man and to bring him into contact with Himself. *The Christian faith teaches men not to repudiate the material world, but to* use *it.*

The essential quality of a sacrament, then, is that of an 'out ward and visible sign' conveying an 'inward and spiritual grace.' In the early days of the Church, an attempt at a systematical classification of sacramental action was made. But from the beginning two sacraments stood out—Baptism and the Eucharist—as being 'dominical,' or instituted by our Lord Himself. To them, the Middle Ages added five others, to complete the mystic number seven—Confirmation, Penance, Unction, Holy Orders, Matrimony. The more extreme reformers denied the name of sacrament to these last five; but the Prayer Book was content to define the two great sacraments of the Gospel—Baptism and the Eucharist—as alone 'generally necessary to salvation'; while not specifically denying the claim of at least some of the others to the title.

A. *The Eucharist*

Of the two great dominical sacraments, the Eucharist is given pride of place in the Prayer Book. For Baptism, the Sacrament of Admission, can only be administered once in the case of any one person, and may therefore rank as an occasional service; whilst the Eucharist, the sacrament of Fellowship and Sustenance, needs to be continually received afresh by all. It is as much part of the common life of the Church as family meals are of the home. The Eucharist, however, is not only a pledge of brotherhood and a means of spiritual refreshment: it is also a memorial sacrifice, in which the Church, obeying her Divine Master's dying command, makes 'remembrance' of His sacrificial death upon the Cross and pleads the merits of that sacrifice in union with His own perpetual presentation of it in Heaven before the throne of God. *It is thus the supreme expression of the basic idea of all Christian worship: that only through Him who is our Head in Heaven can the Church on earth properly make its own approach to God.* So it takes rank as the supreme act of worship, to which all other worship is subsidiary. The pre-eminence of the Eucharist in Christian worship does not belong to it just because it is the oldest service of all, or because it is the only one that rests upon the Lord's command, or because in it Christ comes to the believer in a particularly intimate way. These things are all true. But more important still is that it is the Eucharist which provides the key to *all* worship. That is why it is placed in the centre of our Prayer Book.

It may well be asked, however, was this what the compilers of the Prayer Book meant? Did they intend the Eucharist to occupy this great position?

When at the Reformation the Church of England gave to her people the great blessing of a Liturgy in the mother tongue, she had no intention of cutting herself adrift from the history and experience of fifteen centuries of grace and devotion, any more than she had any intention of severing her connection with the Catholic Church, or of ceasing to teach the Catholic faith. She purposed to continue the offering of that sacrifice of praise and thanksgiving which Jesus had laid down for His Church when He said: 'Do this in remembrance of me.' Continuity was not lost because the services were translated into English and simplified. At the present time, the Roman Catholic Church is simplifying her services, and translating them into the tongues of the people. Nobody is suggesting that she is thereby breaking continuity with the past.

A word which illustrates the Church of England's purpose of continuity is 'sacrifice.' Prior to the Reformation, the word 'sacrifice' as applied to the Eucharist had been greatly abused and was thus much disliked. In her peculiar position, the Church of England might have decided that it would be better to drop the word altogether; she was undoubtedly greatly tempted to do so. Instead, she deliberately retained it—both in her Catechism and in her Liturgy. She tried to restore the biblical meaning of the word, for in the Bible the word means 'life offered to God'; and to strip off from this biblical word the medieval superstitions that had gathered round it.

The Church of England condemned such 'sacrifice for masses, in which it was commonly said that the priest did offer Christ for the quick and the dead, as blasphemous fables and dangerous deceits' (Article 31). But nowhere does the Church of England condemn the doctrine of the Eucharistic Sacrifice, and indeed she teaches it. In a famous papal bull, *Apostolicae Curae* of 1896,

Pope Leo XIII argued that the Church of England was not part of the Catholic Church because she did not believe in the Eucharistic Sacrifice. In a famous reply in the year following, Archbishop Temple of Canterbury and Archbishop MacLagan of York stated emphatically that the Church of England both held and taught the doctrine of Eucharistic Sacrifice.

The Church of England is anxious to safeguard the uniqueness of the Sacrifice of Calvary. We sing:

'Once, only once, and once for all
His precious life He gave . . .'

'One offering, single and complete,
With lips and heart we say.'

That is Anglican teaching, copied from the Prayer Book: 'Who made there by his one oblation of himself, once offered, a full, perfect and sufficient sacrifice, oblation and satisfaction for the sins of the whole world.' There is but one life worthy to be offered in sacrifice, but one life worthy to be accepted. But that offering was, and is, 'for us,' that is, on our behalf. We, too, must offer ourselves; we must not stand outside Calvary as spectators only of that all-sufficient sacrifice. Somehow we must come within its scope, adding our lives to His, so that He, our great High Priest, can offer them along with His own.

And it is He Himself who makes this possible. For at the Eucharist which He ordained and which, by His appointment, we celebrate, we keep His command, 'Do this in remembrance of Me,' when we take and bless, break and distribute the bread as He did; the bread which He called His Body. At each Eucharist He stretches out His hands to us, and into those hands we place ourselves and our lives. Look again at the Prayer Book words:

> 'We entirely desire thy Fatherly goodness, mercifully to accept this our sacrifice of praise and thanksgiving. And here we offer and present unto thee ourselves, our souls and our bodies, to be a reasonable, holy and living sacrifice, unto thee . . .'

What words could be plainer than those?

To offer myself, however unworthy, is my 'bounden duty and service.' The Prayer Book puts into words the dilemma of the worshipper who knows himself a sinner and who yet must worship:

> 'And although we be unworthy, through our manifold sins, to offer unto thee any sacrifice, yet we beseech thee to accept this our bounden duty and service, not weighing our merits but pardoning our offences, through Jesus Christ our Lord.'

So Cranmer translated the Latin Canon—the words that had been used at this point in the Western Church from the very earliest days. Dr. William Bright in 1873 also translated them in the words of a well known hymn:

> 'Look, Father, look on His anointed face,
> And only look on us as found in Him.
> Look not on our misusings of Thy grace,
> Our prayer so languid and our faith so dim.
> For lo! between our sins and their reward
> We set the passion of Thy Son our Lord.'

That is the Catholic doctrine of the Eucharistic Sacrifice as taught in the Church of England. Such a doctrine seems also to be evangelical in the real sense of that much abused word.

But such worship must be consummated in service. By itself, it is not enough. What we vow with our lips must be performed in our lives. The first step, the first essential step, is to make the vow, and to make it publicly. It is very much like marriage, which begins with a vow made at the altar, but it only begins there; it must go on to be completed in life and living. Just so, worship begins at the altar with a service which contains a vow of self-dedication, the service of the Holy Eucharist. But that vow is consummated in service, in a life devoted to God and to one's fellows. 'Worship is not merely a service; it is service.'

But how are we to grow in service?

To that question the Christian gives this answer—'By the grace of Christ's own sacrifice, which is given to us in this blessed Sacrament.' This brings us to the question, *'What, if anything, is given to us in this Sacrament?'*

At the Reformation there were many professors of a new doctrine; they would say quite sincerely, 'Nothing is actually given to us in the Sacrament itself, but by eating bread and drinking wine, as our Lord commanded, we are reminded of what He did for us on Calvary; and when we are thus reminded (or when we thus remind ourselves) we stir up the grace that is in us.' In other words, the Sacrament is not a 'means of grace' but a reminder of grace that has already been given in another way.

This was new doctrine, hitherto unheard of, but one which the Church of England was very tempted to accept; for the Church reacted very strongly from some of the materialistic views which had been common in the later Middle Ages. Nevertheless, in spite of the temptation, the Church kept steadfastly to the Catholic teaching that in and through this Sacrament a real gift of grace is given. In the Catechism, she teaches her children that the receiving of this Sacrament is 'generally necessary to salvation,' and 'generally necessary' does not mean 'necessary as a general rule, but can be done without in special cases.' It means 'Necessary for the whole race (genus) of mankind, universally necessary.' She goes further, to teach her children to say that 'The Body and Blood of Christ are verily and indeed taken and received by the faithful in the Lord's Supper.' The words of Article 28 are stronger still. There the Church teaches that 'the Body of Christ is given, taken and eaten in the Supper of the Lord.' It is true that this is qualified by the statement 'only after a heavenly and spiritual manner,' but this does not in any way weaken the directness of the teaching concerning the reality of the Gift, and that for two reasons. First the Body of Christ is a spiritual reality, and could only be received in a spiritual manner. Secondly, the Church of England would teach, in common with the rest of Christendom, that 'the spiritual' is 'the real,' much more real than the material. So many people seem to think that 'real and actual' means 'material,' whereas 'spiritual' means 'unreal and imaginary' —'the stuff that dreams are made of.' But the Bible uses the words in the opposite sense. For example, 'God is a Spirit' surely does not mean 'that God is unreal and imaginary.' St. Paul tells us that 'The things which are seen are temporal, but the things which are not seen are eternal.'

The earlier part of Article 28 makes the matter quite clear. There the Church states:

> 'The Supper of the Lord is not only a sign of the love that Christians ought to have among themselves one for another; but rather it is a Sacrament of our Redemption by Christ's Death, insomuch as . . . the bread which we break is a partaking of the Body of Christ.'

It is a partaking of, not a reminding of, the Body of Christ. *Thus, in the controversies as to whether any Gift were given or not in this Sacrament, the Church of England came down emphatically on the traditional and Catholic side—that there is a real gift, really given, and really present to be given.* For 'that which is verily and indeed taken and received' or 'given, taken and eaten' must be a Real-Thing-in-Itself, and not merely an idea in the mind of the receiver.

One might have thought that this wise and careful teaching would have settled the question four hundred years ago. But alas, in spite of the plain words of the Prayer Book, there has persisted the idea that the Eucharist is only a memorial of the Death of Christ, instead of being a sharing in His risen life.

The subjective teaching that the Presence of Christ in His own Sacrament is dependent on the faith of the receiver still persists, as though, if we *believe* Him to be there, He *is* there; but if we do *not* believe Him to be there, or cease to think of His Presence, He is no longer there. In other words, the miracle of Christ's own Presence in His Sacrament would not be wrought by His own action in accordance with His promise, but by our faith! What happens if both believers and unbelievers attend the same service? Is He present to some, and not to others? And if so, what is meant by 'presence'?

Worse still, there are those who think that this is what the Church of England officially teaches, and some even claim that 'modern psychology' endorses it. Now, it is true that some modern philosophers, called 'pragmatists,' seem to teach that it doesn't matter what you believe so long as you believe it. Thus, 'if I believe in God, then for me, there is a God' and 'if you do not believe in God, then for you there isn't a God.' But this means that God's existence depends on my faith; it reduces God to an idea in my mind; and in fact it reduces all human thought to absurdity. It is in fact intellectual suicide.

For God is the One who made the world, and upon whom the whole universe depends. That's the meaning of the word 'God'; to go on to say that God depends for His existence or His presence on my belief in Him is madness.

The folk who say this do not believe in God at all. And the people who take the subjective view of grace, and talk as though it were a kind of 'auto-suggestion' do not really believe in grace. They believe in themselves and in their own power to get 'better and better every day and in every way' without God and without His grace.

But the Church does believe in God, and in God's grace, and in the reality of Christ's presence in this Blessed Sacrament. He is there, whether we are there or not, whether we are reverent and attentive or irreverent and inattentive, whether we believe or disbelieve. His presence is REAL—independent of us and of our faith, outside us, beyond us or above us. He is present in the Body broken and in the Blood shed; and He is there not at our will or by our command. He is there at His own will, in accordance with His own promise; and we are there by His command to greet our King. It is good that we should acknowledge His presence with reverence and godly fear. It is good that we should stretch forth our hands in faith and lift up our hearts in loyalty to welcome Him. But let us make no mistake about it. The Church of England teaches (in common with the rest of Catholic Christendom) that the sin of an unworthy Communion lies in the fact that it is the Very Body and Blood of Christ which we receive unworthily.

The Church of England teaches, then, that the Holy Communion is a real gift of grace, and not merely a reminder of grace. The actual phrases 'means of grace' and 'as a means whereby we receive the same' are Prayer Book terms. Let us ask then, *What is this Gift?* There again the Church uses the scriptural and traditional terms and the presumption is that she uses them in the scriptural and traditional sense. The Gift given, she says, is 'the Body of Christ'; 'the Blood of Christ.' She uses these terms in the Catechism and in the Articles; and also in the Words of Administration. As he gives Communion the Priest says, 'The Body of our Lord Jesus Christ which was given for thee' and 'The Blood of our Lord Jesus Christ which was shed for thee.'

What do these words mean? Again, the Church of England was very careful to guard against medieval error—in this case a philosophical explanation of the mode of the Real Presence which, she said 'overthrew the nature of a sacrament.' But by her use of the traditional terms and by her refusal to give them up, she shows that she means to continue to teach her people that they receive in this Sacrament what the Church had always taught, and what all Christians had hitherto believed—namely, Christ Himself in all His fullness, the Christ who had died, but who now was risen from the dead. That is, 'Christ risen, ascended, glorified.' In the sixth chapter of St. John's Gospel, we find the Eucharistic teaching of our Lord Himself—taking as His text the Feeding of the Five Thousand. Then, as now, men find it difficult to believe that He means what He says, and they ask 'How can this Man give us his flesh to eat?' (John 6: 59, 60). Here is the answer, and it is His own answer. This is the way in which He gives us His flesh to eat, and He Himself devised it. It is Himself that our Lord consecrates for us, Himself that He gives to us, in the Blessed Sacrament, and on the Cross, once in time on earth, and in the heavens eternally—Himself, His Body and His Blood, the human nature that He shares with us; and it was in order that He may share human nature with us that He took human nature of the Blessed Virgin Mary, when He came down from Heaven and for us men and for our salvation was made man.

In the sixth chapter of St. John's Gospel, Jesus tells us why He devised this plan. 'Except ye eat the flesh of the Son of man, and drink his Blood, ye have no life in you.' Here, then, He gives us His Flesh and Blood that we might have life, and might have it abundantly; that we may share His own life, and so have the grace to live as He lived and die as He died—that is, sacrificially—'for the sins of the whole world'—and to rise again as He did, triumphantly.

In her Catechism and her Articles the Church teaches us that the Sacraments are not only pledges to assure us that we receive grace, but 'are the means whereby we receive the same'; that they are not only reminders of grace, but 'effectual signs of grace, whereby he doth work invisibly in us' (Article 25). An effectual sign is a sign which effects or brings about the things it signifies. The overhead cables of the Grid system are not merely signs that electricity is being supplied; they are the actual carriers of the current. In the same way this Holy Sacrament is a means of grace, the actual vehicle by which the grace of God is given to our souls.

Because therefore the Church teaches that a real gift of grace is bestowed through this Sacrament, she insists in the Catechism that it is 'generally necessary to salvation' and like Holy Baptism 'of great necessity where it may be had.' It is not a devotional extra, or a spiritual luxury for the pious few, nor is it a token of such as be already assured that they are saved. *It is the necessary Bread of Life, as necessary to souls as ordinary bread to bodies.* If men do not believe this, it is not the Church but our Lord Himself whom they refuse to believe. If they will not come for the Bread of Life, they have only themselves to blame if they do not receive It. And their unbelief does not make the promises of Christ any the less true, or make ineffective His provision.

'Generally necessary' means 'necessary for the whole of humanity.' Christ did not give us this holy Sacrament at such cost to Himself that we may be free to use It or refuse It as we like. This Sacrament is Christ's hand outstretched to us; if we refuse it, it is His outstretched hand that we refuse. So again, the Church of England sought to teach her folk to come more often to this Sacrament, and to prepare for It more carefully than they had done in the past.

Finally 'Communion' which is a Latin word, or 'Koinonia' which is the Greek, means fellowship. This Sacrament, given by Christ, is to be the effectual sign of the unity of His Church. In other words, Holy Communion is meant to be the cement with which He binds into one the 'living stones' with which He is building His Church. Therefore the Church has always regarded the Bishop of the Diocese as the proper person to be the minister of this Sacrament, since the Bishop is the Apostolic representative of Christ, and the father of the family of the Church. In practice, however, it is celebrated by a Priest, as one, that is, who is ordained by the Bishop to a share in his pastoral oversight of the faithful.

Here at the Table of the Lord the Family of God meets; there is no precedence; we all eat the same spiritual meat and we all drink the same spiritual drink. Christ Himself presides at this Feast as the Host; He Himself is the Priest at His own Sacrifice; it is He

Whose love divine,
Gives the guests His Blood for wine;
Gives His Body for the Feast,
Christ the Victim, Christ the Priest.

That hymn was one of the earliest and most widely used in Christendom, and comes down to us from the seventh century.

B. *Holy Baptism*

The other great Gospel Sacrament is that of Holy Baptism. At the Reformation, the Church of England kept the practice of infant Baptism as performed in the Early Church. It was regarded as reasonable that the children of Christian parents should be brought 'within the Covenant' as soon as possible; though the growth into the graces of the Christian calling could only come as time went on. In addition, the practice of infant Baptism clearly proclaimed that divine grace was not something *earned,* but freely given by God of His own free love. Baptism is the beginning of the Christian life, not its crown, as is perhaps suggested by the Baptists.

But the Prayer Book clearly intends that only those children shall be baptized who have a reasonable chance of growing up to lead a Christian life. Thus an important place is assigned to godparents. Parish priests are often distressed by the superstition surrounding the indiscriminate use of the sacrament; and the situation in which 67 per cent of all children in this country are baptized in the Church of England, and only 23 per cent brought to Confirmation, shows clearly that much more careful preparation of parents and godparents is needed, as well as 'public' Baptism, often in the presence of the congregation. In populous parishes, it may well be that the re-siting of the font, away from its traditional position by the south-west or west door, is called for. To place the font at the east end of a side chapel, balancing and level with the altar, at once emphasizes the dignity of the sacrament and makes administration much more visible and dignified. The administration of Baptism is clearly designed to be a solemn public act, performed in the presence of the congregation. Whilst practical difficulties in large parishes would make it difficult always to honour the rubric, which directs that the service shall be performed 'immediately after the last lesson at Morning Prayer, or else immediately after the last lesson at Evening Prayer,' nevertheless it is only fitting that the congregation shall be properly represented to receive the new members. If this is not so, the Church is clearly to blame for perpetuating a situation entirely contrary to the Prayer Book's intention. *We must never forget that in the early days of the Church, Baptism was an occasion of immense solemnity and dignity performed in the presence of the faithful.* This is the ideal we must aim to restore, as indeed the Reformers tried to do.

The Catechism that follows Baptism and precedes Confirmation so logically in the Prayer Book stands in close connection with them both. At Baptism, godparents are told to see that their godchildren are taught 'all that a Christian ought to know and believe to his soul's health,' as a preparation for Confirmation. The Catechism is the Church of England's summary of the knowledge required before Confirmation.

III. 'OTHER RITES AND CEREMONIES OF THE CHURCH'

All of these presuppose the two great sacraments of the Eucharist and Baptism as their accompaniment. They are designed for use in the case of baptized persons only. Confirmation opens the door to Holy Communion. The 'other Rites and Ceremonies'—Holy Matrimony, Visitation of the Sick, Burial of the Dead and the Churching of Women—are intended to be administered in connection with the Eucharist, however little this may now have come to be the case.

(i) The Order of Confirmation is really an integral part of the Sacrament of Baptism which it completes. In the early days of the Church, Baptism was followed immediately by the gift of the Holy Spirit through the laying on of hands by the Bishop. This was followed at once by the reception of the first Communion, even by infants. Later on, the fact that the Bishop was seldom present at a Baptism made it necessary to postpone Confirmation, and therefore first Communion, to a later period. The Prayer Book lays down no definite rule as to the age of Confirmation, beyond saying that candidates must have come 'to a competent age,' or 'to years of discretion,' and must be instructed in the Faith. To-day, the usual time is between thirteen and fifteen, corresponding with the adolescent years. There is a good deal to be said for Confirmation either at an earlier age or a later one.

Though described as a 'rite' and not as a 'sacrament,' Confirmation is obviously an expression of the sacramental principle. In this case, the 'outward and visible sign' is the laying on of the Bishop's hands, and the 'inward and spiritual grace' is the gift of the Holy Spirit. It was not instituted by our Lord, but it is definitely apostolic and has been practised ever since a few years after our Lord's ascension (Acts 8: 17). Finally, it is vital to emphasize that Confirmation is something done *to* a person, not *by* him.

(ii) Solemnization of Matrimony

Unlike other Sacraments and rites of the Church, marriage is not purely ecclesiastical in character. It existed as a Divine ordinance long before the Church existed: the religious ceremony is secondary to the natural compact. But from earliest ages marriage has been accompanied by religious rites. The blessing of God and His Church has from the beginning been regarded as having a sacramental character, giving a definite grace for a fulfilment of the married state.

The apparently abrupt ending of the service is to be explained in the light of the rubric which reads: 'It is convenient that the new-married persons should receive the Holy Communion at the time of their Marriage, or at the first opportunity after their Marriage.'

(iii) The Visitation of the Sick

From its earliest days the Church has laid great stress upon the duty of visiting the sick and the dying. With this help and comfort was associated the practice of anointing, partly for healing, partly to bestow forgiveness. Though since 1549, the Church of England has *officially* abandoned the practice of anointing, there has been a great modern revival of the Ministry of Healing, which can still make use of parts of the Office of the Visitation of the Sick, though it is seldom nowadays used in its entirety. Certain parts of it are extremely valuable, in particular the fine 'commendatory prayer for a sick person at the point of departure.' The sick person is to 'be moved to make a special confession of his sins, if he feel his conscience troubled with any weighty matter'; and the Priest is directed to absolve him in a translation of the old Latin Absolution, couched in personal terms quite different from the general terms used in the daily Offices and the Eucharist.

Here then, *the practice of private Confession receives definite sanction from the Prayer Book,* as it does in the direction, given in the first Exhortation in the Communion Office, to the effect that 'if there be any among you who . . . cannot quiet his own conscience . . . let him come to me, or to some other discreet and learned Minister of God's Word, and open his grief; that by the Ministry of God's holy Word he may receive the benefit of absolution, together with ghostly counsel and advice . . .' However, in both cases, the responsibility of seeking absolution is left to the sinner himself. The Church of England says: 'All may; none must; some ought.'

The Office for the Visitation of the Sick is followed by a form of service for the Communion of the Sick. At the present, however, following the ancient practice of the Church, the alternative method is often used of giving Communion to the Sick with the elements consecrated at the celebration of the Eucharist in Church and 'reserved' for the purpose, in an aumbry or tabernacle.

(iv) The Burial of the Dead

In the early Church a service for the burial of a Christian meant much joy; but in the medieval Church the rites associated with the burial of Christians had become gloomy, elaborate and penitential. The Prayer Book Office is scarcely an altogether inspired one, retaining only selected parts of the old services, and dropping altogether the 'Requiem' celebration of the Eucharist, as from 1549—though its Collect is transferred to the service at the graveside.

Parish priests in very large numbers have used the great enrichment provided by the new or alternative material in the 1928 Prayer Book—so much more convenient, liturgically acceptable and helpful to the mourner. The 1928 book also provides an alternative for use when the burial is that of a child. Subsequent recent revision has continued to provide helpful guidance.

(v) The Thanksgiving of Women after Child-birth, commonly called the Churching of Women

Giving thanks after the birth of a child was known among the Jews as 'Purification,' a name also used in the 1549 book. The rubric at the end directs that 'if there be a Communion, it is convenient that (the woman) receive the Holy Communion.' Hospital Chaplains may offer the present thanksgiving service whilst mothers are still in the maternity home; otherwise the priest should be asked as soon as possible after return.

(vi) A Commination concludes the 'occasional' section of the Prayer Book. For use on Ash Wednesday and other days as appointed, it is designed as a substitute for the solemn public penance, so much a feature of the early Church. The solemn 'cursings' taken from the Pentateuch find no echo in modern worship and the 1928 Prayer Book has greatly altered this part, without changing the point of the service, which is to emphasize God's horror of sin and judgment of it.

The main body of the Prayer Book also includes two other vital sections to be used in conjunction with services. The first of these is set between the daily Offices and the Eucharist, and stands in relation to both—*the Collects, Epistles and Gospels* to be used daily throughout the year. The second section contains the *Psalms of David,* placed after the Occasional Offices and designed for use in connection with the daily Offices. Together, they have formed a large part of many Christians' devotional reading; and have had a formative effect on the character of the Anglican Churchman.

IV. 'THE FORM AND MANNER OF MAKING, ORDAINING AND CONSECRATING OF BISHOPS, PRIESTS AND DEACONS'

The Church's minister must be properly authorized and it is necessary that he be 'ordained' by those in authority to do this in the name of the Church. The Church is 'apostolic,' that is, its government was entrusted by its Lord to His chosen Apostles, who in their turn handed on their powers to others, and so on through the ages.

So, in addition to his calling to the ministry—his vocation—he must also receive the solemn authorization of the Church 'by publick Prayer, with Imposition of Hands.' In this, too, a special gift of the Holy Spirit is imparted (as in the case of Confirmation) to equip him for his ministry.

The Church of England accepts the threefold division of Bishops, Priests and Deacons, which seems to have become established in the Church in the earlier part of the second century; it does not recognize the five 'minor orders' which came into existence subsequently—sub-deacons, acolytes, exorcists, readers and doorkeepers. So the Prayer Book provides for the 'making' of deacons, the 'ordering' of priests and the 'consecration' of bishops. All are performed by bishop or bishops. For the consecration of a bishop, three bishops at least are required; in the clerical directory, *Crockford,* the names of all bishops present at a consecration are inserted, so important is the Apostolic succession thought to be. *In all three services, the ordination is inserted into the Communion Office—which has, from beginning to end of the liturgy, been the backbone of the Church's Offering.*

THE ALTERNATIVE SERVICE BOOK 1980

A tremendous event took place in the Church of England's life when in 1980 *The Alternative Service Book* was produced. Here is a whole range of alternatives for use in our Church in conjunction with the Book of Common Prayer, together with the Liturgical Psalter. For the first time since the Act of Uniformity, the balance we attempt to hold in word and sacrament is expressed in two books, rather than in one. We have, then, a vastly important supplement to the Prayer Book; and the addition of a date to this remarkable new book is a reminder that it will probably be revised at regular intervals, as has indeed been the case in other parts of the Anglican Communion – such as the Scottish Episcopal Church and the Church of Canada – where notable 'up-to-date' prayer-books have been available for many years. Indeed, adaptation of the Church's worship should be a continuous process, for any liturgy is a child of its own period.

It is now widely accepted that unity needs no longer to be marked by strict uniformity in liturgical practice. In consequence, the provision of Alternative Services in modern language is seen as a great enrichment to the life of the Church, for patently the 1662 Prayer Book was unable to provide for some of the needs of the present generation. The 1980 book was the result of considerable experimentation in revised forms during the two previous decades, in which virtually every parish in the land had been involved. The debate between 1965 and the publication of the book was intense, and continues to excite interest.

Under the terms of the Worship and Doctrine Measure, 1975, the 1662 Book of Common Prayer retains its authority as a doctrinal standard, therefore. But now its riches are greatly enhanced by a revision which commands increasing respect, as this century draws to its close; and, as its preface says, 'in the hope that GOD's people may find in it a means in our day to worship Him with honest minds and thankful hearts.'

Further reading:

Charism and Sacrament (Donald Gelpi, SPCK).
A Handbook of Parish Worship (Michael Perry, Mowbray).
Priest or President? (Harvey, SPCK).
The Psalms: A new translation (Bickersteth, Collins).
Pray Every Day (R. Jasper, Coughlan, D. Jasper, Collins).
The Vision of God (Kenneth Kirk, James Clarke & Co., Cambridge).
Study Acts 2: 38; 8: 1–22; 9: 1–19; 10; 11: 15–17; 16: 14–40; 19: 1–6 in all regarding Christian initiation.

Discuss:

What aspects of the Holy Communion are emphasized in some of its other titles—Holy Sacrifice, Lord's Supper, Liturgy, Mass, Eucharist?
Choosing godparents.
Confession of one's sins is the starting-point of Christian living.
Marriage has been given in Reformed theology a dignity equal to the state of dedicated celibacy.
The minister of the Sacrament is a channel of grace only, otherwise no man of a humble heart dare seek Ordination.
In the sacrament of Unction, we pray for wholeness of body, mind and spirit; whether we get well or whether we die, we believe that the grace of the sacrament will bring us nearer to God.

APPENDIX II

SCHEME OF SACRAMENTS

Sacrament	Outward and Visible Sign	Inward and Spiritual Gift
1. Holy Baptism	Water and the sign of the Cross	New birth of a member of Christ
2. Holy Communion	Consecrated Bread and Wine	Souls fed by Christ's Body and Blood
3. Confirmation	Laying on of hands	Strengthened by God the Holy Spirit to become a full member of the Church
4. Penance	Confession of Sin and Words of Absolution	Forgiveness of Sins
5. Ordination	Laying on of hands	Strength to minister conferred by God the Holy Spirit
6. Marriage	Agreement to be man and wife until death and giving of a Ring	Grace given to live well in marriage
7. Unction	Anointing with consecrated oil	Healing of body and mind

CHAPTER V

The Church's Faith as Taught by her Seasons

(a) ADVENT

THE Church watches and waits for the second coming of Christ. On the day of Ascension, now many years ago, He vanished out of the Apostles' sight, but the Church believes that one day He will come back. And the Church believes this because He said that He would—in His teaching to the Apostles, when He told them the parables of the talents and the ten virgins; also He assured the High Priest that He would return when the High Priest challenged Him to say whether He persisted in His claim to be the Messiah. Our Lord made the dramatic answer: 'I am, and ye shall see the Son of man sitting on the right hand of power and coming in the clouds of heaven' (Mark 14: 62). And the angels at the Ascension promised the same thing when they said to the Apostles: 'This same Jesus which is taken up from you into heaven shall so come in like manner as ye have seen him go' (Acts 1: 11).

The promise that Jesus made, and that the angels confirmed, has not yet been fulfilled, nor do we know when it will be, because neither He nor they have said; but the Church believes that it will be, and lives her life accordingly.

During the season of Advent we think a good deal about our Lord's Second Coming. The word 'Advent' means 'coming.' If you go out to seek adventure, you go out to seek whatever may come. Originally the season of Advent was merely a preparation for Christmas, as Lent is a preparation for Easter, but it soon came to stand for more than that. As Church people thought about our Lord and His coming to Bethlehem, they could not help thinking also about His Second Coming, wondering when it might be and what it would be like. The Creed says that when our Lord does come a second time, He will judge the quick and the dead. Whether that will be pleasant or unpleasant for us will depend upon our spiritual condition. When a judge comes to a law court, innocent people regard his coming with calm satisfaction. They hope to have their cases dealt with and their wrongs put right. Only people with guilty consciences are afraid, and it will be like that with our Lord's Second Coming. Only for the unfaithful and the hostile will it be a day of anxiety or fear.

(b) CHRISTMAS

Everybody, at least everybody in this country, we hope, is familiar with the story of our Lord's birth at Bethlehem on the first Christmas Day, but not every one knows the reasons why it took place. In the main there are two. The first was this—*our Lord was born in order that He might make to God a great apology for human sin.* Good men had felt sorry for their sins many times before Jesus came. But they had always felt that their sorrow was somehow not real enough or deep enough. It was not that they felt that God was demanding that they should show greater penitence than they did, but rather that they felt that God was so holy that He deserved to have a better apology than any that they themselves could make. There was a second reason—God wanted people to have a new and better opportunity for living in union with Him. In Old Testament times, people had had opportunities of coming near to God in the tabernacle and the temple. But God wanted people to have an opportunity of coming to Him nearer still, and if men were to be able to come nearer to God, it was necessary that God should first come nearer to men. Men could never come from sin to God unless He gave them special opportunity.

These purposes continue by the continued self-offering of Jesus in Heaven and by the continued presence of Jesus in the Holy Sacrament of the Altar. When the Catechism asks the question: 'What is the inward part or thing signified in that Sacrament?' the answer is made: 'The Body and Blood of Christ which are verily and indeed taken.' Jesus is 'taken' in the Holy Sacrament because He is already there for that purpose.

A very practical question is 'What shall we do personally on Christmas Day?'

Christmas Day, so the Prayer Book reminds us at the head of the Collect, Epistle and Gospel, is the Nativity of our Lord, or the Birthday of Christ.

Lots of people do nothing about it. They decorate their houses and buy a lot of presents and eat a lot of food, but that is not exactly celebrating Christ's Birthday. If I, on your birthday, were to arrange for myself a private feed somewhere, I could not very well say that I had kept it. I might have enjoyed the food, but I should not have kept your birthday. On a birthday one has to do something about the person whose birthday it is and direct it towards that person.

We find an answer to our question in the word 'Christmas' itself. 'Christmas' is a sort of concertina word. It is two words compressed together—'Christ' and 'Mass.' It is a day for the special celebration of Christ's Mass, in recognition of the great purposes for which Christ was born—it is a day when we delight to attend the service in which, above all others, the same purposes of the Incarnation are realized.

(c) EPIPHANY

The Crib

Those of you who have been brought up as members of the Church will have seen many kinds of Christmas Cribs. All over the world there are Cribs, small and great, each with their own distinctive beauty. We have most of us been into churches where from cheap and simple materials, from straw and brown paper and Christmas tree frost and a couple of old packing-cases, a Crib has been made, often very beautifully. We have also seen costly and expensive Cribs with figures of great beauty and worth, such as that to be seen in St. Paul's Cathedral and in many other places. But always the main note of the Crib is a simple one, matched by the simple people present—a shepherd or two picked up at random from the fields, and a carpenter who has been refused a night's lodging, and his wife and baby—anybody who wanted models for a set of Crib figures could find them at the nearest workhouse.

A Change of Scene

Then comes the Feast of the Epiphany and we go to church to find that there has been a disturbance and a re-arrangement in that familiar group in the stable. There are camels and elephants, outlandish beasts; there is a negro bringing a foreign note into the picture; there are rich and royal clothes; there is pomp and pageantry; there are exclusive gifts lying on the edge of the straw.

Few stories have exercised such a hold on the imagination of Christians as that of Epiphany, and it is a story that we of the present generation would be ill-advised to neglect. There is no doubt that nowadays the thought of men and women and the things that they do in their daily lives are controlled by natural science. What is perhaps less certain is the benefit that it gives in hard terms of human happiness. In the days of our great-grandfathers it was thought that the reign of science must begin a time of great peace and plenty and of clear thinking and understanding. Nowadays we realize that this is not true. We know now that it began a period of increased tension and there are hints that worse may yet follow.

The Lesson of Epiphany

The only answer to the difficulties in which we find ourselves depends on the attention that the world gives to the lesson of Epiphany. *The Magi, or wise men, were scientists,* skilled in the knowledge of their day and particularly in astronomy. As used by them, however, it was not the kind of master that led its servants to destruction. On the contrary, it guided them to the fuller knowledge of God and to the feet of the Infant Christ. *The Magi were kings, too.* They were men of power in their own countries. And we live in an age of power, as well as of science. The doctrine of naked power has never been preached more than to-day, and was never accepted without question over so large a part of the world. Rulers of past ages were never armed with such overwhelming power as present-day Big Threes or Fours or Fives, or whatever number it may be at a particular time. The very achievements of science have placed unparalleled resources of power in the hands of the central authorities of the State.

The Consecration of Power

Epiphany is a parable of the way in which power should rightly be used. Three kings come in their splendour and lay their offerings at the feet of a mightier King. The amazing thing is that this king, whose sovereignty they acknowledge, is a new-born babe, the son of Mary. By their obeisance they confess that the earthly ruler, however powerful, has a greater overlord, a master whose authority does not depend upon naked force, but upon the more spiritual claims of law, justice, morality and love.

The Search for Unity

This age is also one that searches desperately for unity. Never were the disasters which follow on lack of unity so obvious or so formidable. *The abiding message of Epiphany is one of unity.* The kings who followed the star represent different nations. Yet, as they kneel before the Crib, they are united, and the humble shepherds join with them—the workers of the earth with the rulers of the earth—and the dumb creatures add their presence. All are united by a fellowship in worship. What a fine presentation of the Christian religion is here! Before the Babe in the manger, who is King of kings and Lord of lords, differences fall away and they are at one with each other.

It is in this way alone that unity comes to men. Between nations it will only come about when rulers and parliaments of different countries freely recognize the authority of the Divine Law, and confess that the Justice of God is more important than the self-interest of their own particular country; beween classes it will spring from the recognition that God's love is given freely to all men, in creation and redemption; between members of one family it comes when the Crib is made the centre of the home, and the Infant Saviour is adored by all. *The only unity that is real and permanent is the result of humble submission to the Babe of Bethlehem and the determination to obey His will for the world.*

(d) LENT

The 'Gesima' Sundays

The three Sundays immediately before Ash Wednesday—the 'Gesima' Sundays—are called Septuagesima, Sexagesima and Quinquagesima. The names are Latin and they mean seventieth, sixtieth and fiftieth. They are given to these three Sundays because they are roughly seventy, sixty and fifty days before Easter. These Sundays help us to get used to the change from the glad season of Epiphany to the hard-working season of Lent.

Lenten Thoughts

During Lent we think of the sadder side of our Lord's life and in particular about His temptations in the wilderness and His crucifixion. The season starts by turning our thoughts to the one, and ends by turning our thoughts to the other. But we do much more in Lent than think of the sad side of our Lord's life. *We think about the sadness that our Lord suffers now because men displease Him and disappoint Him still, and not least about the sadness that He suffers now because we ourselves sometimes hurt Him in those ways.*

But the season of Lent brings to the instructed Christian good cheer, for the word 'Lent' comes from the Anglo-Saxon word 'Lencten,' which means quite simply 'Spring' or 'Growth.' Although the winter may not yet be over, the coming of Lent is a welcome reminder of the coming of Spring, and the re-awakening which we see in Nature at the same time should be echoed in the renewing of the life of the soul.

Ash Wednesday and Shrove Tuesday

The first day of Lent is Ash Wednesday, which derives its name from the distinctive ceremony belonging to that day, a ceremony that used to be widespread in the Church and which is still maintained in a number of places. This is called 'The imposition of ashes.' The congregation kneels at the altar rail and the priest passes along, carrying a small bowl of ashes made of burned palm leaves left over from Palm Sunday the year before. As the priest passes before each person, he dips his finger lightly into the ashes and then makes the sign of the Cross with his thumb on that person's forehead, symbolizing the new start in Lent, just as the sign of the Cross in Baptism symbolizes the new start of life.

We cannot very well dedicate ourselves to God, however, if we have any unforgiven sin on our consciences, so before Ash Wednesday comes another important day, Shrove Tuesday, so called because our forefathers used to call getting absolved by a priest 'being shriven.' In preparation for Lent, therefore, the Church provides in her wonderful calendar this day for those who are in need of the sacrament of penance to seek out the priest and receive God's absolution after solemn confession of one's sins.

Lenten Planning

The season of Lent lasts for forty days, excluding Sundays which come in between, because Sundays are always festivals. They do not count as days of Lent. There are Sundays *in* Lent but not *of* Lent. A long period of time, such as forty days, requires some planning if it is all to be used to the best advantage, and we need to plan both what we are going to do and when we are going to do it. In the main we should aim at five things: *We should aim at getting more control over ourselves by giving up something that we like; we should aim at saying some additional prayers, preferably in church after communion; we should aim at some additional almsgiving; we should aim at some additional Bible-reading; and we should aim at some additional church-going.*

In this connection it is right, at this time, to realize again that worship at the altar, private prayers and the study of God's Word are all most important parts of the life of the Christian. That is why each should be remembered and 'spring-cleaned' in the Lenten rule. As Christians, we have the duty to bear witness to our Divine Master, and we best do this when we continually review the rule of life by which we live.

One of the devoted men of God of this century was Charles Gore, the saintly first Bishop of Birmingham. Throughout his whole life he was a power of righteousness. After his death one who knew him well wrote: 'When I think of him, a lump comes into my throat and I bow my head.' Another wrote: 'Though I have had many tutors in Christ, he was, above all others, my father, and in so far as I can picture Jesus Christ, I picture him as not unlike the father I have lost.' Charles Gore was a man who, above all, governed his life by a strong and noble rule which he reviewed from time to time, and what these men wrote about him, is, after all, an illustration of the simple yet profound truth that *the best argument for God is the life of a good man or of a good woman.*

Of the scientist Clerk Maxwell it was said: 'He made faith in goodness possible to other men.'

We may recall also that in the Acts of the Apostles it says of the first Christians that 'Men took knowledge of them that they had been with Jesus.' Their life was such that it could not be explained away but by the fact that they had been touched by the life of Jesus. Certainly these early Christians ruled themselves rigidly in their Christian lives in a way that would make some modern Churchmen gasp. If you want to see how they did this, then look at Acts 2, verses 42–7. As you read that you will see that it is all governed by the word, in verse 42, 'steadfastly.' What they did was done, not now and again, but day after day, by rule. Through this came their strength and work of witness in the world. *To help others to believe in God and His goodness by the force of personal example is the vocation of every Christian.*

You may recall the memory of a friend who, by his character, so often put us to shame and made us long to share in his goodness, and many of us owe much in this way to those who influenced us in our early years. 'No man liveth unto himself,' and whether we like it or not, each one of us is a power in the world, either for good or for evil. We may be successful or unsuccessful in life as the world counts these things, but we shall certainly not have lived in vain if, in future years, someone can say of us, 'I am so glad I knew him, for I am a better person in consequence.'

History tells us that Lent was originally a season of preparation, during which candidates were prepared for Baptism and Confirmation, which were principally administered in the early Church at the great festivals, particularly on Easter Eve. So it has become the custom of the Church to make use of the Lenten season in a similar way, by seeking to know and extend the Faith to which we are professed, as followers of the Divine Master. That is why, in most churches, special services are arranged during Lent, more particularly of an instructional nature, and all thinking Christians should seize the opportunity given for learning more of the Faith.

Obedience and Love

Some people do not care for Lent. They like Christmas and Easter and Whitsuntide, and the other great festivals, but they do not care for Lent. Lent tests us in two things, and few people like to be tested. It tests our loyalty. The Church, like every other society, has her rules, and those rules her members ought to be ready to obey, not merely when the rules are pleasant, but when they are not so. Otherwise, they are letting down their profession as Christian men and women. Keeping Lent is one of the Church's rules. Lent also tests our love. It is possible to do something with perfect obedience and yet, at the same time, to do it most unwillingly. We do not want our Lenten obedience to be of that poor quality. So whatever we do during Lent by way of Lenten observances should be done with this thought, that we are doing it to show God our loyalty and our love. Go to your parish priest for guidance in special reading and amendment to your rule of life if you feel you need help.

(e) HOLY WEEK

Holy Week begins on Palm Sunday, and it is the one week out of the whole of human history of which Christians possess a detailed diary. You will notice one big feature about the stories of the week. As far as our Lord is concerned, this was a planned week. Deliberately He faced it and went through with it. To begin with, on Palm Sunday He rode into Jerusalem amidst all the cheering, and proclaimed Himself Jesus of Nazareth, King of the Jews. You will remember that He rode on a donkey during this triumphal entry into Jerusalem. The whole point of this is that Eastern kings rode on horseback when they came to make war, but when they came to make peace they rode a donkey sidesaddle. So, by approaching Jerusalem in this way, Jesus of Nazareth proclaimed Himself King of the Jews, threw down the gauntlet and rode on to meet the consequences.

The people, caught up with emotion, hailed Him as a leader who would make the Jewish nation great. But our Lord, in the four days that followed, quickly dispelled their illusions. 'Straightway,' the Gospel tells us, 'he entered into the Temple and began to cast out them that sold, saying unto them, "It is written—and my house shall be a house of prayer, but ye have made it a den of robbers." ' St. Luke's account goes on significantly: 'And he was teaching daily in the Temple. But the chief priests and the scribes and the principal men of the people sought to destroy him; and they could not find a way to do it, for the people hung upon him, listening.' Chapters 20 and 21 of St. Luke's Gospel are full of our Lord's wonderful teaching during those fateful four days.

Maundy Thursday

Then, later in the week, on the Thursday in the evening, He offered to His friends those amazing mysteries of His Body and Blood in the Bread and Wine. 'Continue to do this,' He said, 'in remembrance of me.' 'And then he went out,' says St. Luke, 'as his custom was, to the Mount of Olives, and the disciples followed him.' And these were our Lord's best men, for the shadow of the Cross was upon Him. He chose them to help Him through, just as we ask for the prayers of our dearest friends when we are against a crisis. Our Lord endured great agonies of indecision inside Him. 'Father remove this cup from me if it is possible; nevertheless, not my will, but thine, be done.' But those three best men fell asleep; like others before, and since, their spirit was willing, but they lacked the energy and vigilance which being a follower of Christ requires.

Good Friday

The consequences of it all led, as our Lord knew they would, to the Hill of Calvary on the first Good Friday.

Underneath Him stood a centurion who must have been used to crucifixions from many previous occasions and would, therefore, have known what to expect—the shrieks for mercy, the hysterical curses, the raving to God for vengeance on the executioners. But the behaviour on this occasion was sufficient to change this rough man for the rest of his life. What first drew his serious attention to this supposed criminal was that He did not shriek or curse or cry for vengeance. Indeed, He did not seem to be thinking of Himself at all, for He kept on murmuring, 'Father, forgive them, for they know not what they do,' and, after a time, when He was conscious of His mother as she stood there watching, He said, 'Mother, go home now. John will look after you.' To such an onlooker as the centurion, it was all very strange from a man who was dying in agony. Certainly one of the thieves put to death with Him thought so, for he glanced at the notice that a cynical Roman governor had nailed over Christ's head and he said: 'Saviour, think of me when you come into your kingdom.' In the circumstances, don't you think that was an extraordinary piece of faith for one dying man to say to another? And the reply was an even more extraordinary piece of faith: 'My dear man, I assure you that *to-day* you will be with me in Paradise.'

The effect on the soldier who saw and heard was, probably for the first time in his life, to move him to pity that this young prince should come to so untimely an end. But gradually, as he stood there, he realized that he was being moved by something far deeper and more disturbing than pity. The last words came, words of complete trust: 'Father, into thy hands I commend my spirit,' and then the head drooped forward, and the centurion saw that the end had come. For some moments he stood speechless. Then the others heard him say, more to himself than to them, 'Truly, this man was the Son of God.' And, as he spoke, the darkness that had covered the earth since midday began to lift. The centurion's words heralded the first faint gleam of returning day—of a new day, of a new kind of day, a day whose full, fresh glories and deathless dawn we commemorate each Easter Day, with hearts uplifted.

These words of the centurion should mean a great deal to you and to me, because in the greatest drama ever staged, the centurion was playing the part of the ordinary man and woman, seeing the Cross of Christ for the first time. During those three dreadful hours, his whole idea of life was turned upside down and back to front. You know that famous hymn which originally began 'When I survey the wondrous Cross, where the young Prince of Glory died, my richest gain I count but loss, and pour contempt on all my pride'? That is what the centurion was doing. He was realizing that his whole sense of values up to this had been false; that this derelict figure was indeed a King; that the Cross of His agony and humiliation was also His throne; and the crown of thorns was really a Royal Diadem.

The Bridge

It is not true that Christianity has been tried and found wanting; it has been found difficult and not tried. When Christ died on the Cross, He completed God's bridge to us. Before that, there was a gap between ourselves and God, and only if God has crossed to us can we hope to cross to Him. Deliberately He came over to our side of the gap to share the pain and evil of our lives here, and now He offers us the Bridge of His own Life, so that we may, in our turn, cross to God. *'My life,'* He was saying, *'is offered, offered for mankind to share and to use, for I am come that they might have life and have it more abundantly.'*

Our response to that, if we really mean business, includes owning up to our sins which make the gap; it includes a firm intention to live, in other words to *use,* the life which is the bridge across the gap; it includes regular and reverent reading of the Bible; and prayer; and faithful attendance at the Holy Communion service and on other occasions of Christian worship.

At heart, it is as simple as the faith which you put in any bridge-builder when you walk across his bridge.

(f) EASTER

The story of Easter begins where the story of Good Friday leaves off—that is, in the garden of Joseph of Arimathæa. This Joseph of Arimathæa was a rich Jewish counsellor who came forward late on Good Friday afternoon to beg the body of Jesus from Pontius Pilate, and to offer his own sepulchre for its burial. A sepulchre was a cave cut in a rock, partly natural and partly artificial. Inside there was a narrow shelf upon which a body could be laid, and outside there was a round stone, something like a millstone, turning in a groove to form a door.

Our Lord's burial was a very hasty business, because there was so little time between His death and sunset, and everything had to be finished by sunset. He died at about three o'clock in the afternoon. Then there was some delay while Joseph of Arimathæa went to Pontius Pilate, and still more while our Lord's death was verified to the governor's satisfaction. That was why the women came to the sepulchre on Easter morning. They wanted to make the burial arrangements more complete. They did not come on the Saturday, the day in between, because that day was the Sabbath and, therefore, a day considered unsuitable.

The Empty Tomb

When the women arrived, they found the stone already rolled away, and the angels inside the sepulchre told them that our Lord was risen and that they were to inform the others. The women ran away to do as they were told. They seem to have scattered as they went, and gone in different directions, for only one came to tell Peter and John—that one, of course, was Mary Magdalene. When Peter and John heard the news they ran off to the sepulchre, and we have a full account of it in the Gospel for Easter Day. It is important that we fully realize what is meant by the words about 'the linen clothes lying' and 'the napkin that was about his head, not lying with the linen clothes, but wrapt together in a place by itself.' It means that our Lord's grave clothes were found lying undisturbed, just as they had been placed with His Body inside them on Good Friday afternoon. *It means that when our Lord's Body was transformed from a physical body to a spiritual body in the process of Resurrection, it had passed through and out of the grave clothes without disturbing them.* It was a Jewish custom, when burying a dead body, to put one set of wrappings round the body and another set round the head. The two sets would lie in separate positions after His Resurrection had taken place.

The First Appearance

The discovery of the empty tomb was not the only exciting thing that happened that day. Mary Magdalene, after going with the news to the house of Peter and John, made her way back to the garden. She was too curious about it to think of going home, but too much out of breath to run with the Apostles, so she came to the garden a second time, but only after the Apostles had gone away. There and then it was that she saw the risen Jesus, the first of the disciples to do so. It is a significant thing that our Lord appeared first after His Resurrection to a woman who had been an outcast sinner amongst her own people, and who had been utterly without hope before our Lord befriended her.

Other Appearances

Some time after this appearance to Mary Magdalene, our Lord appeared to Peter, when and where we do not know, but possibly soon after Peter had returned from the garden and possibly at his lodging-place. Then, the same afternoon, as two disciples were walking along the road from Jerusalem to Emmaus and were talking over the puzzling events of the morning, Jesus approached them, talked to them and went with them. They did not know Him but felt strangely uplifted by His company, so much so, that when they reached Emmaus they asked Him to stay the night with them. He agreed to do so, but as they sat down to their evening meal and our Lord pronounced a blessing over it, they recognized Him and He vanished from their sight.

Finally, the very same night our Lord appeared to the Apostles in Jerusalem. They were gathered together, probably in the house of the Upper Room, discussing the happenings of the day so far as they were known, and expecting any moment to have officials call to enquire what they might know about the disappearance from the sepulchre of our Lord's body. To their great relief, no officials came, but to their intense delight, our Lord did.

Part of the message that the women carried from the angels in the sepulchre to the Apostles was that the latter were to go into Galilee, and that our Lord would meet them there, and after a slight delay, caused by the unbelief of Thomas, they went to Galilee, and there Jesus *did* meet them. Seven of them, finding the strain of waiting very heavy, went fishing on the lake, and in the early morning, as they returned, they saw Jesus standing on the shore. Some time after that, Jesus appeared among the mountains to a great gathering of disciples, more than 500 of them, who were especially assembled for the purpose. It looks as though Jesus made the arrangements for this gathering when He appeared to the seven Apostles by the lake.

His Followers Learn the Truth

So the disciples and the Apostles gradually learned that Jesus was indeed risen from the dead, and eventually the Resurrection of Jesus became an essential article of the Creeds. In the Apostles' Creed it is put 'The third day he rose again from the dead.' Sometimes you may wonder why it is put 'the third day,' when Easter Day was only two days after Good Friday. This was because the Jews and the first Christians reckoned days inclusively, that is, they reckoned in the Friday as well as the Saturday and the Sunday.

The doctrine of our Lord's Resurrection is a tremendously important one for two reasons. First, it proves that *our faith in Jesus is justified.* All that He said about Himself, and especially about His divinity, is true. Neither man nor death shall be able to crush Him. Then His Resurrection assures us that *so long as we hold to Him, neither man nor death will be able to crush us.* In due time we shall die, but in due time also we shall have a resurrection. We do not expect it to be quite the same as our Lord's Resurrection, with all the particles of this body transformed, but we believe that sufficient of this body will be raised from death to enable us to recognize ourselves and one another.

(g) THE ASCENSION

After His Resurrection, Jesus made a number of appearances to His disciples, as we have already seen. Why is it that these appearances were made? First, perhaps, we may say that *He wanted to reassure His disciples as to His being alive, and also He wanted to give them further instructions as to what they were to do.* But these appearances could not go on indefinitely because there were two things that Jesus wanted to do in Heaven and two things that He wanted His disciples to do. *In Heaven our Lord wanted to resume His heavenly glory, and to present Himself there as the great apology for human sin.*

When the Jews offered a sacrifice in ancient times they did so by presenting to God the blood of some animal. They killed the animal first in order to obtain its blood, but it was the animal's blood, rather than the animal's death, that they regarded as their sacrifice. So Jesus, having been slain on Calvary and having risen from the dead, now wanted to present Himself in Heaven as the eternal equivalent of a sacrificial animal's blood. In other words, *Jesus wanted in Heaven to be a king and a priest.* But He also wanted His disciples to do two very important things. *He wanted them to be His witnesses and He wanted them to receive the power of the Holy Spirit for this purpose.* He told the Apostles about these two things in the upper room on the night before His crucifixion, and the account is given in the Gospel for Ascension Day.

Forty days after His Resurrection Jesus made one last appearance to the Apostles in Jerusalem. He led them out of the city, over the hill called the Mount of Olives, and in the direction of the village of Bethany. Somewhere on the far side of the hill, as the path went down towards the village, He gave them one last solemn farewell. Then He raised His hands in blessing, and disappeared from their sight in a cloud. This time our Lord had gone from them finally. For weeks now He had been appearing to them at different times and disappearing, and they had never known from one day to another whether He would come or not. Now they knew that He would not re-appear in this form again, but they were not sad about it. *On the contrary, they were very glad, because our Lord had said that He would always be with them* (Matt. 28: 20), *and after He had gone they received the promise that one day He would return* (Acts 1: 11).

The Church commemorates our Lord's Ascension on the Feast of the Ascension, which falls on a Thursday forty days after Easter. The Festival of the Ascension is a great occasion in the Church. It ranks in importance with Christmas and Easter although many people, who talk about Christmas and Easter when these seasons come round, do not realize that the Ascension is equally important. *Remember that it is the feast of the coronation of our Lord, a day of obligation to Communion for every confirmed Christian, and a day that should be kept with full Christian observances.*

(h) WHITSUN

The word 'Whit-Sunday' is a shortening of 'White Sunday.' That seems to be a strange name for a Sunday when the colour of the altar hangings and vestments is red, but it is so called because this Sunday, years ago, used to be a special day for Baptisms and Confirmations, and the candidates for these sacraments commonly wore white robes for the occasion. This Sunday is also often called the 'Birthday of the Church,' because it commemorates the start of the Church in the time of the Apostles. There is an exciting account of what happened in the Acts of the Apostles, 2: 1–41.

The disciples had been waiting in Jerusalem as Jesus had told them to do when He left them on Ascension Day. They were to wait, He said, for the coming of the Spirit. What the Spirit was, they then scarcely knew, but they did understand that He was to be Someone divine and Someone distinct, although not separate, from the Father and Himself; and Jesus said the Spirit was to come 'not many days hence.'

The Spirit is Given to the First Disciples

Early on the tenth day after the Ascension, on a day that happens to coincide with the Jewish Feast of Pentecost, the disciples were startled to hear a sound like a fierce wind, although there was no wind. There came a flash of light which seemed to divide into pieces, and over the head of each of them there appeared what looked like a little flame. At the same moment each of them felt himself to be filled with a new and wonderful spiritual power. They told themselves that this was what Jesus had promised.

The crowd that gathered on account of the noise naturally wanted to know the reason for the strange happenings, so Peter stepped forward and spoke for himself and his friends. He said, 'Some of you think we are drunk because we are so excited, but we are not'; and he went on to tell them how Jesus, after His crucifixion, had risen from the dead and ascended into Heaven, and had now just sent down upon His followers the Spirit whom He had promised. Many of the people who heard Peter give this explanation began to feel that, in the crucifixion of Jesus Christ, a great wrong had been done, and they wanted to know what could be done about it now. Peter said that they must do two things. They must repent and then they must be baptized. If they did that, then they also would receive the gift of the Holy Spirit. *So many people took Peter at his word that, whereas up to that moment the number of disciples had been only about 120, it now rose to 3,000. In this way the Church began.*

The Holy Spirit in the Church

We profess our belief in the Church when we say in the Apostles' Creed—'I believe in the Holy Ghost, the Holy Catholic Church, the Communion of Saints, the forgiveness of sins, the resurrection of the body, and the life everlasting.' We have to say those words all together, because they go together. It is the Holy Spirit who made the Church and who invigorates it. It is in the Church that we enjoy the Communion of Saints and the forgiveness of sins. It is through the Church that we begin to live the everlasting life.

The term 'Church' sometimes means a living thing (a collection of people belonging to it), or a lifeless thing (a building of bricks and mortar in which they meet). In the former case we usually say 'The Church,' and write the word with a capital 'C.' In the latter case we commonly say 'a church' and write the word with a small 'c.' Originally the word came from a Greek word 'ecclesia,' which we still use in the form 'ecclesiastical,' and which means 'the people called out.' It was a very suitable name for the society of our Lord's friends, because the members of the Church were people who were definitely called out by Him in a special way and for a special purpose.

Why is it that the Church is called 'Holy' in the Creed? Simply because it is the creation of God and is intended to be holy. Why is it called 'Catholic'? Because it is intended to be in all places and to include all people and to teach all the truth that is known about God. The word 'Catholic' is another Greek word and means 'complete.' So the Church's membership is designed to be complete and its teaching is to be complete.

The Foundation of the Ministry

So the Church started in Jerusalem; and very soon it began to spread. But now, not every new member was baptized by an Apostle. Often it happened, as new members were so numerous, that they were baptized by some assistant of the Apostles and only confirmed by the Apostles—that is, the Apostles laid their hands upon the heads of the people baptized (Acts 8: 14–17). However, whether the new members were baptized by the Apostles in person, or baptized by their assistants and confirmed by the Apostles afterwards, all of them received a share in the gift of the Holy Spirit, and they received that gift so that they might all be witnesses for Jesus.

Before Jesus went back to Heaven, our Lord said that He wanted His disciples to be His witnesses and that He would send them the Holy Spirit for the purpose. 'Witness' to Him is a very important part of the Christian life. He said He wanted His disciples to be witnesses unto Him 'both in Jerusalem and in all Judæa and in Samaria and unto the uttermost parts of the earth' (Acts 1: 8). As the original disciples would never live long enough to get to the uttermost parts of the earth, His saying made it clear that He expected those who became disciples after Him to carry on their work.

Church people to-day are still able to receive the gift of the Holy Spirit by the laying-on of the hands of the Apostles' successors, who are the Bishops, in the sacrament of Confirmation, and *we receive this gift of the Holy Spirit in this way so that we, too, may bear witness to Jesus as the first disciples were expected to do. We share their gift and we also share their duty.*

(i) TRINITY

Trinity Sunday is the festival that the Church holds each year in honour of the mystery of God's being. We have to say 'mystery' because, although we know a certain amount about God, we have not the mental faculties necessary for knowing everything about Him. It sums up the rest of the Church's Calendar.

The Development of Belief

Far back in ancient times people believed in many gods—gods of the hills, gods of the rivers, gods of the seasons, gods of the nations and many others. Then very gradually they began to learn that there is only one God, and that the many gods in whom they believed were imaginary and false. The first people to learn this were the Jews, and they learned it because the only true God taught it to them through their prophets, so that they might make it known to other nations. There was, however, another truth about God that God wanted men to know. *He wanted them to know that in the one Godhead there are certain mysterious distinctions.* God did not expect them to learn how it is there are these distinctions—that would be quite beyond human understanding—but He did want them to know that there are the distinctions, and whereas the first lesson was taught through the prophets, the second lesson was taught in a much more wonderful way—by the coming of Jesus. Jesus came into the world and spoke about the Father and about the Son and about the Holy Spirit. The terms were those that He Himself used, and evidently they represent distinctions in the Godhead, because *Jesus spoke of the Father and of the Son and of the Holy Spirit, each of them as being Divine, and each of them as being distinct, and yet none of them as being separate from the others.*

Distinctions in the Godhead

The Jewish people found this second lesson very difficult to learn. As we know, they eventually put Jesus to death. Our Lord's own disciples found it very difficult to learn also; but they were willing to learn it. In that they were greatly helped by what happened on one very remarkable day when our Lord was being baptized in the river Jordan. As Jesus was standing there in the river with St. John the Baptist standing by Him pouring water over Him, a voice was heard from Heaven. 'This is my beloved Son,' and a dove fluttered down on to our Lord's shoulder. The voice was the voice of Him whom Jesus called the Father, and the dove was the Spirit taking, for the moment, a bird form, and Jesus Himself standing in the water was the Son (Mark 1: 1–11). So gradually the disciples accepted the idea that in the one Godhead there are these three distinctions. We have a special term to describe this idea of the distinctions in the Godhead—it is the term 'Trinity.'

The Church's Teaching of the Trinity

The word 'Trinity' is made up of two words joined together, the one 'tri' and the other 'unity.' So we have 'trinity,' or 'tri-unity,' or 'three-oneness.' We find the term made use of and defined in the Athanasian Creed. Reading from the third verse we find this: 'And the Catholic faith is this, that we worship one God in Trinity, and Trinity in Unity, not confounding the persons (that is, not confusing them), nor dividing (or separating) the substance, for there is one person of the Father, another of the Son, and another of the Holy Ghost; but the Godhead of the Father, of the Son and of the Holy Ghost is all one, the glory equal, the majesty co-eternal (that is, of the same endless duration).'

The Catechism relates the work to each person of the Trinity in turn—to the Father, it relates the work of creation; to the Son, the work of redemption (*or the liberation of men from the power of sin*); *to the Holy Spirit, the work of sanctification* (*or the process of becoming holy*).

Actually they are all together in one person of the Holy Trinity, themselves all different; but it helps us, the Catechism seems to think, to learn about them in this way.

St. Paul made use of the same method when he wrote the lovely benediction, 'The *grace* of our Lord Jesus Christ, and the *love* of God, and the *fellowship* of the Holy Ghost, be with us all evermore' (2 Cor. 13: 14).

The Catechism says that we *believe* in the Trinity, and, quite honestly, that is all that we can do about anything so mysterious; for everything that belongs to God's Inner Being is necessarily quite beyond our human understanding.

Further reading:

I want to be a Christian (Packer, Kingsway Publications).
Holy Spirit (Michael Ramsey, SPCK).
The Atonement (J. W. C. Wand, SPCK).
Handbook of Christian Belief (Lion Publications).

Classwork:

The Class should compose a joint Calendar for the Church's Year, with the help of Prayer Books. If use of colours for seasons is made, the completed work might well be passed on to the Sunday School Superintendent as a visual aid.

Discuss:

What are we to say to a dying person who is fearful of God's Judgment?

Jesus was born to make a great apology to God for us.

Is unity amongst Christians (a) desirable, (b) possible?

Could a Rule of Life lead to becoming 'mechanical' in the things of God? Are there worse dangers?

Only the knowledge of our perpetual need of mercy can enable us to extend unselfconscious forgiveness to others.

The followers of Jesus tried to believe anything else until the truth of the Resurrection was forced upon them.

If we believe Jesus has gone to prepare a place for us, why are we so reluctant to speak of death?

The Acts of the Apostles is the story of the Spirit-filled community. (Read especially 13: 12–52; 15: 1–28; 16: 6–10.)

'Far from being remote or theoretical, the doctrine of the Trinity is the most practical thing on earth because it shows us that God, the Absolute, infinitely removed from the nothingness of creatures is yet not unattainable.'

CHAPTER VI

Growing in Holiness

THE SPIRITUAL LIFE

ANY advice on the spiritual life ought to stress our potential usefulness to God because only if we put the emphasis in the right place shall we understand what the spiritual life is about. It is a life that grows day by day in usefulness to God by becoming more and more abandoned to Him and so more and more a vehicle of grace.

In leading this life, we often begin by making a great mistake—that is, that it depends on us. It does not. It depends upon God. If we can grasp this truth, prayer, which is an important element in the spiritual life, would not seem so laborious a business. The initiative prompting us to pray comes from God. We pray because He speaks to us. Miss Olive Wyon writes in her excellent little book, *The School of Prayer,** 'It is not we who originate prayer. It is God, the Holy Spirit, who makes us want to pray. It is He who moves us to worship. It is He who teaches us to pray.' Though we would discredit the notion, many of us believe that God died on Calvary in A.D. 33. Yet Easter is a perpetual reminder that His work of creation and redemption has never ceased. He came down and was born in a stable in Bethlehem, and He is still coming down. Though we are not always in His presence He is always in ours. St. Paul wrote to the Romans, 'The Spirit helpeth our infirmities, for we know not how to pray as we ought, but the Spirit himself maketh intercession for us with groaning which cannot be uttered.'

The first thing which we must realize, then, about the Christian life is that it does not depend upon our own frantic efforts, but upon our response to what the theologian calls the prevenient grace of God. And by that is meant, quite simply, whether we accept or reject Christ as our Saviour when He reveals Himself unmistakably to us—as He always does. The spiritual life begins when, for the first time, we catch a glimpse of the love of God, and that may happen to us quite suddenly when we are alone, or when we are in the company of someone whose life is Christ-filled, or when we are reading a book. It may happen when we are young or when we are old. It may be that we are given only one such experience or many. But when it comes to us, when we feel for the first time this absorbing love of God within us, we know by instinct that life without this as our constant possession is meaningless. 'I count not myself to have grasped, but as one *that has been grasped* I press on,' says St. Paul. That is the only thing we can do to respond to this gift and to make the act of will necessary.

This act of will in response to the love of God is called conversion, and is the only possible beginning to the spiritual life. But there is a danger in the word 'conversion,' for it tends to suggest that once we have made this initial surrender of ourselves to God, the rest will be plain sailing. Whereas, of course, we know, out of our experience, that for the rest of our lives we shall be called upon to make acts of the will, abandoning more and more of our human nature to God.

It is here that what is called moral theology can assist us, for the great teachers of the spiritual life—St. John of the Cross in particular—show us that there are three stages in the potential progress of every man. These are called the way of purgation, the way of illumination and the way of union.

Do not be frightened by these technical words. The Church of England has lost much by its mental laziness. It is not enough to live by the parable of the Good Samaritan. A vague Good Neighbour policy is insufficient. The spiritual experience of St. Teresa, of St. John of the Cross, of Von Hügel and many others, can enlarge our lives enormously, for through them God the Holy Spirit speaks as surely as He does in the Bible. St. John records words of our Lord which make it clear that only a part of the truth, perhaps only a small part, was recorded in His ministry—'I have yet many things to say unto you, but ye cannot bear them now,' and so on, throughout St. John, Chapters 14–17.

These three stages of the spiritual life are exactly what our own limited experience would lead us to expect. First there is the way of purgation, which means, of course, cleansing. This is the phase in which, though we have made our initial surrender to God, we are still troubled by serious temptations which sometimes overcome us. To put it very simply, we honestly want to be Christians, and for a time we are, and then suddenly we strike a bad patch and we give way to the world, the flesh and the devil.

Many of us never pass through the way of purgation, but if we do, we come to the way of illumination. In the way of purgation there is a more or less constant tension between the claims of God on the one hand, and the claims of our own human nature, only partially redeemed, and of the world on the other hand. In the way of illumination this struggle is over; the tension is resolved; we grow gradually in the love of God as He enlightens us step by step. Our desire for Him is habitual, not sporadic; our knowledge of His truth and love is immeasurably increased.

Then finally we may come to the way of union, in which the whole mind and heart and will are from moment to moment in touch with His mind, His heart and His will.

As you read this, you may perhaps be thinking, 'What has all this to do with me? No doubt this is admirable for monks and nuns, and even for the laity in a more leisured age, but how is it going to make me more useful to God?'

If we can see the glory of a life lived in absolute union with God (and surely our own fragments of experience together with the compelling converting power of the lives of the saints *can* help us to see this) then we shall desire to pass on from the purgative way to the illuminative way. What are the stages by which we pass from one to the other?

Look first at the Passion, and then at the teaching of the masters of the spiritual life, and see what counsel they give us. These leaders tell us that if we would grow in the knowledge and love of God, three things are necessary: mortification, habitual recollection, and humility. Let us look at each of these in turn.

Mortification is a word which many of you will not know, yet there is no better word for it. It means the deliberate surrender of things that please our bodily senses. It is what our Lord means by fasting; only we have restricted the meaning of that word to abstinence from food and drink. Our senses, sight, smell, taste, hearing, give us enormous satisfaction. We enjoy our food. We enjoy the theatre. We enjoy television. We enjoy a lovely garden. And there is no reason why we should not enjoy God's good gifts.

Yet often we enjoy these things so much that they lead to over-indulgence, and our love of them takes the place of love of God. Mortification is the deliberate giving up of what we enjoy with our senses as an act of love towards God. This is what some do in Advent and Lent, and what we all ought to do at times in and out of Advent and Lent. Mortification also consists in the deliberate acceptance of dull, distasteful and even painful duties as a means of growth in the grace of God. *Much of our ineffectiveness as evangelists is because of our refusal to take mortification seriously.* When Jesus was casting out the evil spirit in a man whom His disciples could not heal, he said, 'This kind cometh out only by prayer *and fasting.*' We become filled with the power of God not only when we pray, but when we pray and act. To become possessed of new spiritual life, we must first be prepared to give up that which costs us something. The keen golfer may do more for his own soul and the kingdom of God by foregoing a golf match when he wants to play, than by going to Holy Communion every day for a month.

Habitual recollection means the realization that though there must be set times of prayer, every moment can be a time of prayer. This, too, is necessary if we are to grow in the spiritual life. Our attitude at work and play must be one of constant dependence upon God. We must strive to cultivate the prayerful spirit so that all we do is offered to God. It is said of St. Francis that whenever he went to answer his door, he repeated the Our Father on behalf of the unknown stranger. St. Teresa said, 'I find Him very easily amongst the pots and pans.' If we can learn to approach all our difficulties and all our opportunities in that spirit, we shall soon find that our set times of prayer are far more valuable. So we shall try to pray for the people we meet day by day as we speak to them, or as we write to them, trying to cultivate this habitual recollection of the presence of God.

Finally, humility. This, of course, is a great deal more than the absence of conceit. It is the only possible attitude of the created before his Creator. Its opposite is independence, self-sufficiency, that kind of pride in us which makes us feel we have nothing to learn from God or man. The truly humble man is the man who knows how rotten a sinner he is. He who quite honestly sees nothing wrong in himself, who finds it hard to particularize in the General Confession, is really a wretched person. Growth in humility, as our Lord made very plain, goes hand in hand with growth in adoration. And if there is no adoration in our prayers, there is no humility in our lives. 'Woe is me, for I am undone. I am a man of unclean lips.'

The purpose, then, of the spiritual life is to be used by God, to be used as instruments of His rescuing love. As Evelyn Underhill says, the final test is not seeming very different from other people, but being used by God to make other people different. And the way to do this is by the abandonment of our wills to God, and, within this mortification, the practice of the presence of God and growth in humility through adoration.

Further reading:

Conjectures of a Guilty Bystander (Thomas Merton, Sheldon Press).

God in our Midst (Martin Reith, SPCK).

Discuss:

The purpose of the spiritual life is to be used by God as instruments of His rescuing love.

SOME ELEMENTARY DIFFICULTIES IN THE SPIRITUAL LIFE

The first of the many difficulties in the spiritual life is that of distracting thoughts. Whether we are on our knees, whether we are taking part in public worship, whether we are listening to someone else talking in the pulpit or on the radio or in the schoolroom, whether we are at our bench, or at our desk, complete concentration is incredibly difficult. Thoughts both good and bad come into our minds and tie us up in knots.

How are we to deal with these wandering thoughts? In the first place, just think for a moment why it is that our thoughts wander, whether in prayer or at work. Surely it is because we are not completely absorbed in what we are doing. Our thoughts do not wander—unless our minds are very shallow or our bodies very tired—when we go to see *King Lear,* for example, or the ballet All of us find some activity absorbing, and when we are engaged in it our thoughts do not wander. *So perhaps one of the causes of wandering thoughts is an inadequate desire for God.* What we really need is to be more absorbed in Him. Each person must find out for himself how best to increase this desire. It is often a good thing, when desire grows weak, to make the act of will necessary to procure and read the life of a man or woman whose soul has been set on fire with the love of God, and we find that it deepens our desire—such books as Maynard Smith's *Life of Bishop Frank Weston**; Ellis Roberts' *H. R. L. Sheppard;* Mrs. Paget's life of her husband, *Luke Paget;* Father Curtis's *Father William of Glasshampton;* and many others, including any of the lives of the officially canonized saints.

Then secondly, at least at prayer, do not always regard these wandering thoughts as an evil to be fought. They may sometimes be the still, small voice of God. Here are some wise words of George Snow, in his book, *Letters to a Confirmand.** He says, 'About wandering thoughts, I shouldn't be too sure that they are always a bad thing. Sometimes this is the way God leads one on to something He wants one to see. Next time you find this happening, just stop and see what it is your mind has wandered to—and then see if there is something God wants to discuss with you. I generally find that my mind wanders either to things that are worrying me or to something I find absorbing: and either of these is bound to be a thing that I need to bring to God to see what He thinks about it.'

Another difficulty in the spiritual life might be summed up thus: 'At times I do really feel that I know and love God, but more frequently, when I pray, I feel that I am up against a brick wall. I seem to be talking to myself. I can't see God clearly nor can I feel that He is there.' This state of mind is very common, and the last thing which we ought to do about it is to worry. The real question is this—'How can I grow into a sense of the reality of God?' About this there are several things to be said. First, *a lively sense of the presence of God is dependent upon regular and unselfish prayer.* Too often we pray only when we feel full of remorse and guilt, and this is just self-pity; or when we want something very badly, and this is just selfishness. This is not likely to lead to a lively sense of the presence of God. Again, all the teachers of the spiritual life are agreed in saying that *feelings*

* These outstanding books may well have to be borrowed from public libraries, or long-suffering parish priests; being now out of print.

must not be regarded as the true or only indication of growing holiness. Evelyn Underhill, in a letter, writes: 'You are still far too much inclined to make feeling the test of religion. All that matters is giving ourselves without reserve to God, and keeping our wills tending towards Him. This we can always do: but to *feel* devout, fervent, aware of His presence, is beyond our control.' We sometimes have the experience of feeling the glowing warmth of the love of God, but we must not expect it always. We must be satisfied with the quiet desire to follow Him and be led by the mind and the will.

There will be times also when our inability to realize the presence of God will be so disheartening that we shall be tempted to disbelieve in God. This was the experience of our Lord Himself upon the Cross where, for a moment, He went through the utter desolation of feeling bereft of His Father's presence. 'My God, my God, why hast thou forsaken me?' God does not often allow beginners in the spiritual life to suffer in this way. But nearly all the saints have had such an experience, and it is called by St. John of the Cross, 'the dark night of the senses.' Von Hügel has said something wise about this: 'When there is a sandstorm in the desert, the Arab does not struggle with the situation, but accepts it, lies down in the sand, covers his head with his mantle, and just waits.' This is all we can do. 'Possess ye your souls in patience.' God can't be clear to us all the time. If He were, He would not be great enough to be worshipped.

Further, if you are worried by 'not feeling the presence of God, remember that every one of us is made differently, and we all come to know God and to love Him in separate ways. The approach of some is through the mind; of some through the imagination; of others through the affections. Peter loved our Blessed Lord in quite a different way from John. Our Lord says: 'If ye love me, keep my commandments.' *If we are honestly trying to follow Him, we are loving Him, whether we realize it or not.* The Christian word 'love' has been debased, and does not mean only a movement of the heart; but a threefold movement of the mind and heart and will.

There is a third and final difficulty in the spiritual life which can be summed up as follows: 'Nothing seems to happen. I have been trying to be a Christian for a long time, and I can't honestly say I am any the better for it.' Now the very fact that we say this is proof that we are better for it. *For growth in a spirit of penitence is a sure sign of growth in the spiritual life.* But the apparent lack of holiness is a disquieting fact to both friends and foes of the Church, and there are a number of things to be said about it. Firstly, we live in a world in which everything is done in a hurry, in indecent haste, and this is not God's way either in creation or redemption or sanctity. As an old divine used to say, 'There is nothing divine about hurry; no hurry in anything divine.' God works at what we arrogantly call a slow pace. There is no hurry in nature or spiritual growth in the mind of God. It is significant that nearly all our Lord's parables about the spiritual life within His kingdom are based upon the visible expression of His natural law: seed-time and harvest: corn, wheat and bread; and yet we persist in trying to hurry the growth of the soul in the same way as to-day we try to improve upon creation by artificial chemicals in the soil; and the results of that may not be entirely beneficial. It just does not seem to work. Evelyn Underhill again has said, 'One of the best things we can do for souls is to wait, and one of the worst things is to force the issue. God lets the plant grow at its own pace.' And although the realization of how God works is no ground for complacency, yet it may give us new hope and new inspiration for perseverance if we realize that *the attainment of holiness is step by step, and failure, however shameful, is not necessarily the end of the world. The saints, after all, were the sinners who kept on trying.*

Secondly, we too are in a hurry, and this invariably prevents growth. We are so keen to win our spurs that we persist in doing battle with weapons of our own choosing. *We forget that our Lord spent thirty years in preparing for a ministry which lasted barely three;* and our ministry, yours and mine, would probably be more effective if we spent more time in letting God the Holy Spirit fashion us to His use and less time in being busy about those things which really do not matter very much. As the old proverb puts it: 'Nature gave us two ears and one mouth that we might hear much and talk little.' Much, if not all, of our slowness in spiritual growth is due to the fact that we abhor quiet, are frightened of the stillness, and are too proud to adore God.

Thirdly, nothing seems to happen, we think, because our

prayers are unanswered. Now it is a truism to say that all our prayers are answered, even though the answer is not what we had hoped for, and here, briefly, there are three things to be said. Our Lord never said that whatever we wanted we should have. He said that our requests would be met if asked 'in His name,' that is, according to His will. If we find a petition is not answered as we had hoped, we can be quite sure that the reason is simply because what we wanted was not according to His will, though it may take us many years to learn His wisdom. Then, it is no use to pray, let us say, for deliverance from some sin unless our vague hopes are accompanied by some act of our own will—some mortification.

Finally, our Lord must have known the desolation of unanswered prayer. He must surely have prayed for Judas, and yet His prayer was disregarded. *We can help those we love through prayer, but we can only help by making it easier for them to come to a decision. We cannot break through their own free will.*

Further reading:

Of Water and the Spirit (Alexander Schmemann, SPCK).
Poustinia: Christian Spirituality of the East for Western Man (Doherty, Ave Maria Press, Indiana).
The Influence of John Mason Neale (A. G. Lough).

Discuss:

'Regular and unselfish prayer brings us near to God.'

MENTAL PRAYER

Mental prayer means praying with the mind, though the heart and will come into it as well. There are many books on mental prayer. Two good ones, though they are not simple, are Bede Frost's *The Art of Mental Prayer,** and Father Harton's *Elements of the Spiritual Life.* A much simpler book for beginners is Wilfred Knox's *Meditation and Mental Prayer,** and also to be recommended is Studdert Kennedy's *When Ye Pray.** As we considered

* Obtainable in most public libraries; or on loan from your parish priest, perhaps! All are worth a real search.

earlier, the purpose of the spiritual life is that we shall be useful to God. It is worth using an illustration to illuminate this truth. Imagine an architect who is commissioned by the government to design a new town. He is told in general of the requirements, and he goes away for six months to an island off the west coast of Scotland, where he will be alone, completely cut off from people and things. With him he takes his wife. After a while the plan takes shape. He enjoys the creative work, and always he keeps in mind that he is designing a town for people to live in. His wife shares his enthusiasm and they talk over the plans as he makes them. After six months have elapsed they return, but on the way the architect is taken ill and dies. But the wife does not let her husband's plans drop. She takes them to the Ministry of Works, explains them bit by bit until they are ready to accept them, and she is able to do this because her mind and her heart were so identified with her husband. She knew his plans; she shared his enthusiasm. That was how she was useful to him.

Perhaps this gives us a clue to mental prayer. If we are to be useful to God, then we must know His plans and share His enthusiasm. Or, to put it in another way, *we must be identified with Him so closely that we know His mind and are in union with His heart.* Mental prayer is the way to this merging of our identity with Him, for we think about Him in His attributes or in His ministry. The subject matter of mental prayer is invariably the Gospel or some attribute of God—His justice, His mercy, His humility, His love, and so on. When we are in the presence of another personality, we frequently find ourselves being influenced by their ideas or their mannerisms. We have all experienced that. *What is more likely than that if we reflect upon the character of our Lord or upon incidents from His life, we shall be influenced by Him?* So in mental prayer we bring our minds—memory, imagination and intellect—to bear upon the character of our Lord, so that by this method of reflection our hearts and wills may be stirred to a more complete abandonment to Him, so making ourselves more useful to Him.

So far as the Bible is concerned, the surest and most rewarding method of growing in holiness is to read and consider the Gospels a little at a time. Take a paragraph, a single incident, a healing, a parable, a conversation, a short group of sayings, anything from about three to about twenty verses. First, get the situation into your head. Then divide the meaning of it into three points and consider each point for about five minutes. So, if your passage is Luke 12: 13–15, the three points might be:

(1) the sense of having a grievance against the world or against the family;

(2) the truth that Christianity is not concerned with quantity;

(3) covetousness.

Finally, extract some practical conclusion for yourself from the whole matter.

The parable which follows will do for to-morrow, and will provide ample further material for consideration and resolution.

A longer passage, like the Good Samaritan, might well serve for five days (Luke 10: 25–8, 29–30, 31–2, 33–4, 35–7), and the Prodigal Son might take six (Luke 15: 11–12, 13–16, 17–19, 20–4, 25–8, 29–32). In fact, each verse of the Prodigal Son would give material for as long as one cared to spend on it.

A very good passage for this sort of purpose is Luke 19: 1–10. Bear in mind that 'little of stature' can be made to symbolize for this purpose 'of small spiritual capacity.' Climbing into a tree means taking advantage of an opportunity of coming into some kind of contact with Christ without identifying oneself with discipleship, organized religion, the Church, and, further, being under the impression that our Lord will not know one is there. Then Zaccheus is seen, and the divine subject of tentative enquiry becomes a permanent Guest. Verse 8 contains material for testing most consciences. The phrase 'son of Abraham' in verse 9 may lead to some useful reflection on the necessity of what is called institutional religion, and the value of the idea of the Church. Verse 10 prompts the enquiry, 'for what sort of person is the Christian Gospel chiefly intended?'

Another suggestion is to spend the allotted time for a good many days in considering all the occasions on which Peter is mentioned as in the company of our Lord. Chief of these are his call (Luke 5: 1–11), his Confession (Matt. 16: 13–20), the Feet-washing (John 13: 4–11) and his Forgiveness and Commission (John 21: 15–23).

It is a good plan to imagine yourself to be in the place of the human figure in the story, to suppose that you are the Prodigal, the elder brother, the wounded traveller, the Priest, the Levite, Zaccheus, Peter and so on. It may be that the situation (as in Luke 1: 28) is unique, that the vocation of the person mentioned is very far from being yours, and that the response of the person (as in Luke 1: 46ff.) is much better than you can ever hope to give. But any one can say and mean the words recorded in John 2: 5, and the lesson of the scene of John 19: 26–7 can be learned and executed in any family. In other directions, things like the denial of St. Peter, and even the treachery of Judas, can be used as self-warnings.

The Epistles are not so easy to use in this way. Philippians and 1 Peter are perhaps the easiest, though the ever-relevant 1 Corinthians has the advantage of being about a series of distinct topics. Romans, 2 Corinthians, Ephesians and Hebrews, are all difficult, though they are full of great riches. It is wise to take tiny portions at a time. Modern translations have caused new life to flood through these books.

This is true also of the Old Testament. Much may be gained from Isaiah 6; 11: 1–9, 12; 25; 26; 28, for example, besides the 'Servant Songs'; and Jer. 31: 31–4; Ezek. 37, and many other passages in these great prophetic books, will help any one. The so called Minor Prophets, Job and the Psalms are treasures; and once fairly launched, one goes on making wonderful discoveries.

An excellent Bible for devotional purposes is the Jubilee edition of the British and Foreign Bible Society. It has 2,000 line drawings of accuracy, and prints in heavier type the most helpful parts for study. One thing is certain. It is those who have advanced furthest into the Kingdom of God who know most clearly that they have not come to the end of the Bible as an aid to *Mental Prayer*. No one ever does. No one ever can.

Further reading:

Elements of the Spiritual Life (Harton).

The Wisdom of the Spanish Mystics (Stephen Clissold, Sheldon Press).

Meditations On Liturgy (Thomas Merton, Mowbray).

Discuss:

'Christianity is the religion of all poor devils.'

THE DOCTRINE OF THE SACRAMENT OF THE PRESENT MOMENT

A very great man, whose name you are unlikely to know but whose influence has been felt very much in present-day writing, is de Caussade. Von Hügel, Evelyn Underhill and Archbishop William Temple all owe much to him. De Caussade's great work is called *Abandonment to Divine Providence,* and in the whole matter of the spiritual life, it is important that we should know what he has to say.

Briefly, we can sum up what he writes in two sentences. First, *there is nothing, however small or apparently indifferent, which has not been ordained or permitted by God*—even to the fall of a leaf. This is a tremendous statement: *everything* that happens is ordained or permitted by God. Think out its implications and you will see how tremendous it is.

Secondly, *since this is so, we must abandon ourselves to Him utterly and accept all that happens minute by minute as His will for us.* This is not easy, but it is common sense. So, he writes, 'All we have to do is to accept the will of God as it is made known to us moment by moment in the guise of a duty to be done, a trial to be borne, a joy to be received; in every experience of life, without exception, God comes to us; if we receive Him humbly, we can and will do His will.' This he called his doctrine of the sacrament of the present moment. The word 'sacrament' means God hidden in matter; and de Caussade was saying, therefore, that in every experience of our life God speaks to us, though we may not recognize it. We may resent our pain, or we may use it. We may strive against our environment, or we may accept and use it. We may say, 'If only I could work with Christians; if only my health were better; if only I had not taken so-and-so's advice.' But in all our circumstances God speaks to us. This is the sacrament of the present moment, if we accept our circumstances as such. So Dom Chapman writes, 'One lives in perpetual doubt and ignorance of what God's will is going to be, but not what it is at this individual moment; that we always know, because it is.' So we take every experience and see it to be sacramental—God revealing Himself to us.

It is not easy. It is not easy to see all the people with whom we come into touch in that way. Some of them anger us; some bore us; some we shrink from. To feel that they, too, are children of God is not easy, and yet we must love them. G. K. Chesterton wrote: 'Unless we love a thing in all its ugliness, we cannot make it beautiful,' and we shall only bring ourselves to love them when we pray for them. William Law, in his classic book, *Serious Call to a Devout and Holy Life,* shows how intercession 'amends and reforms the hearts of those who use it,' and describes the change that constant prayer for his people brought about in Ouranius, the village priest. No doubt his pleading for them affected them, but the first thing that it did was to change *his attitude* to them. We have to learn to see God in all His creatures, *to realize that in the hospital of the Great Physician there are no incurable cases;* and this we shall do only if our lives are rooted in prayer. Surely this was the secret of our Lord's concern for the publicans and sinners, the harlots and brigands—the social outcasts of His day. Those from whom we shrink He loved and loves, because their estrangement hurt Him the more, for He knew the image in which they were created.

It is difficult enough to see people as God's children. What about the dull, arduous, tiring, routine jobs that absorb our energies day by day? How hard it is to see that all these things are God's will for us, and to accept Him as sacramentally present in the duties of the kitchen, the answering of letters, the people we pass in the street, the filling-in of forms, the scraping of potatoes, the toughs in the Youth Club. How hard it is to accept minor trials and tribulations, and to turn them into patient acts of love towards God. It is hard, but if we pray, then these too can be occasions of prayer. St. Francis hallowed every simple action of every day with prayer. As he picked up a piece of paper with writing on it, he would say to himself as he did so, 'This is the word of God.' As he opened his door, he would say, 'Thou art the door.' As he lighted a candle, 'Thou art the light of the world.' And if we could make every action of every day speak to us in that way, prayer would be so mixed with life that they would be one and the same thing. Finding Him in every person who comes across our path, in every experience—will gradually impart to such lives a strange unconscious power, and they will be useful to God.

We can apply this doctrine of de Caussade to many other

phases of life: to the problem of pain and to the vital problem of vocation at work. *Suffering, whether physical or mental, makes or breaks us, according to the way in which we accept it—with resignation and trust, or with resentment and cross-querying.* Von Hügel has said that Christianity does not explain suffering, but it does show us what to do with it. There is a short prayer, pregnant with meaning—'Lord, for Thy great pain, have mercy on my little pain.'

Of the problem of vocation in our work there is something to be said. One of the major issues facing the Church to-day is that millions of our fellow countrymen are bored to tears by the work which earns them their daily bread. It is difficult to see how much of the work itself can be anything but tedious. But for those who have the love of God in their hearts, it can be a great opportunity for winning souls to God. For where there are souls, God is sacramentally present, and we can use any environment, however distasteful, as a means of doing Him honour. Evelyn Underhill has written: 'It is not Christian to try and get out of our frame or separate our outward life from our life of prayer, since both are the creation of one Charity. The third-rate little town in the hills, with its limited social contacts and monotonous manual work, reproves us when we begin to fuss about our opportunities and our scope.'

Our starting point was that the purpose of the spiritual life is that we should be useful to God. The Cross points the way, showing us the way of self-obliteration, the way of absorption in Christ. *It is Almighty God's plan that the world should see Christ in us, or not see Him at all.* That is an appalling fact, and *the world will see Christ in us only if there is the Cross in our lives.* What this must mean for each one of us, only we can say—we and the Holy Ghost. It may mean a decision from which we shrink back in fear. It may mean hurting those we love because of a higher loyalty. It may mean the breaking of a friendship or the putting of it on a different level. It may mean many things, but only if we are obedient to the voice of truth and conscience, as we see it step by step, will the world see Christ in us.

And when they do see this, mighty things begin to happen. The fruits of the spirit—love, peace, joy—will shine in our lives, and we shall be useful to God, proclaiming mercy to those burdened with guilt, peace and power to those stricken with fear, healing to the sick in spirit, zeal to the tired, hope to the cynical. How immensely worth while, therefore, it all is. We see the tragedy of people to whom life is the struggle to run away from countless fears, and so much guilt and shame, and we dare not waste and squander the greatest of God's good gifts, which is time. So we throw ourselves at the foot of the Cross, that we may rise with Him, and share with Him in the bringing of a new life into the dead bones. God grant us, therefore, broken and contrite hearts, and with them a hunger and thirst for the things of the spirit and for the souls of men.

Further reading:

Serious Call to a Devout and Holy Life (William Law).
Precarious Living (Martin Israel, Mowbray).
Saints of the Twentieth Century (Brother Kenneth, CGA, Mowbray).
On being a Christian (Hans Küng, Collins).
The Way of the Ascetics (Tito Colliander, Mowbray).

Discuss:

'The world will see Christ in us; or not see Him at all.'

CHAPTER VII

The Church To-day: Situation and the Need

MATTHEW 5: 14a and 16: 'Ye are the light of the world. Let your light so shine before men that they may see your good works and glorify your Father which is in heaven.'

In the summing up of this book, I want to make a big call to those of you who may be preparing for Confirmation or who have recently been admitted to the full membership of the Church by this great Sacrament, and I cannot think of a call made in higher terms than these words of our Lord.

Try to picture the full conception of Church membership—what it really requires of us—a conception so often forgotten or ignored by many in our congregations; but the only one that will make the Christian faith begin to crack the hard crust of indifference in this country and the world.

WHAT OUR MEMBERSHIP MEANS

Whether Confirmation takes place at adolescence or in adult life, it is always true to speak of it as our biggest self-commitment. We carefully examine a definite way of life which, if we take it seriously, is certain to affect every department of it; and when we make this examination we solemnly pledge ourselves to the acceptance of the Christian religion as it is practised in the Church of England, we make its Creeds and its Sacraments our own, and we enter into full membership of the greatest society in the world—the Holy Catholic Church. From now onwards, our Churchmanship is going to be the background of our family and business life; it will colour all our varied relationships and will largely govern our thoughts on the great problems of life and love and marriage and parenthood and death and the hereafter. Surely it is not an exaggeration to claim that so significant a choice may be called our biggest self-commitment.

Unhappily, a large percentage of those who are confirmed year by year have never troubled to face up to their new responsibilities, with the result that between their outward profession of faith and the actual expression of it in life and in conduct, there has been a tragic gap and, what is worse, this half-digested religion seldom makes itself felt in spiritual stomach-ache. Hosts of respectable communicants would probably be shocked and surprised if they were told that their Christianity did not resemble the religion of its Founder, but we have to face the fact that this remains true; and it is a big stumbling block to the spread of the Church's evangelistic work.

There is a prayer of which frequent use is made to-day. It is an exceptionally fine one, but the honest praying of it requires enormous courage and a vast humility:

> 'Teach us, good Lord, to serve Thee as Thou deservest, to give and not to count the cost, to fight and not to heed the wounds, to toil and not to seek for rest, to labour and not to ask for any reward save that of knowing that we do Thy will. through Jesus Christ our Lord.'

Measure your religion against that prayer. Where are you now? Where are any of us? We are not very far, because we make a habit of doing just those things which this prayer tries to help us combat.

Now the undertakings we make at our Confirmation are nothing less than revolutionary. They are the direct opposite of the way of the world and its superficially-attractive scale of values. As members of the Body of Christ we are called to a service which is its *own reward*—nothing else, and of course it cannot be done without the secret behind such lives, and that is a personal relationship to a living and ever-present Christ. That is the first and last condition of true Churchmanship—personal loyalty to a living person, Jesus of Nazareth, the Image of the Invisible God.

Our Duty of Worship

Along with this realization of a supreme divine friendship comes the eager desire to express it in practical terms, and there is no avenue of expression which can compare with that of communicant membership. Our first and most obvious duty and privilege is frequent approach to the altar where we kneel, as Evelyn Underhill so perfectly describes it, 'on the frontiers of the unseen world.' Here we give and receive, we love and are loved, we speak and are spoken to. It is for this reason that the central place of the Lord's own service is desirable in our Church worship. It is the only thing that brings our Christian fellowship into a really worshipping one, and it is a high but perfectly attainable ideal, that all confirmed members of the Church should aim at, to be present at the celebration of Communion on every Sunday and Holy Day, as the Prayer Book requires. Some may think that this is asking a great deal; but, in truth, it is little if our religion is to us the most important thing in the world.

What, after all, is the Church of God and what is its purpose in the world? It is the great society of the baptized, the living and the dead, brought into being by Jesus Christ; a society through which the Holy Spirit moves and works. St. Paul calls the Church, 'The Body of Christ,' meaning that, as at Bethlehem the Second Person of the Trinity took to Himself a human body by means of which to reveal Himself to men, so Christ reveals Himself to the world to-day through that body of people which we call 'the Church'—which is (solemn thought!) you and me. Bv our Baptism we are made members of Christ's Body, the Church, and within that Body we may, if we will, be fed with the grace of God.

It is our *duty,* as members of Christ's Church, to be present at its meetings in church, and in particular at the Lord's Own Service. We must remember that other services in the Book of Common Prayer were never intended to replace the Holy Communion Service. Historically, Mattins came into existence as a service of preparation for the Holy Communion, and Evensong as a service of thanksgiving for it, and, beautiful as both these services can be, they must never usurp the prior place of the Eucharist. It is at Holy Communion that we obey our Lord's dying command, 'Do this in remembrance of me.' It is there that we realize more than anywhere our membership of the family of God. It is hard to understand how any thinking and practising Christian can fail to be present regularly at the service which Christ Himself gave us.

The Church was intended by our Lord to be a family of people united to Him in the power of the Holy Spirit, in the bond of an unswerving love and obedience. The instructed Christian attends Church to worship and not necessarily to be edified or amused, nor do we attend Church that we may feel better for going. The Church is primarily a *worshipping* community—the word 'worship' means 'worth-ship' and to worship means to approach God, not for what we may obtain, but that we may give Him 'our bounden duty and service.' So it is that an instructed Christian will worship Sunday by Sunday, despite the sermon, or the music, or his feelings afterwards, and despite even the man in the row behind.

Our Great Calling

It is only when this side of our life has been put right, and when our duty of worship is being done well, that we shall be able to carry out the work of the Church amongst those outside the Church, who so greatly need the Church's message of hope. We are to be shepherds caring for our flocks and also fishermen casting our nets into the larger waters of the world, in order to land men and women on to the Rock, which is Christ. That two-fold calling belongs not only to priests but to the whole Church. Every member is expected to live and to pray and to work for the extension of Christ's Kingdom by witness amongst all with whom he comes into contact. If you are going to leave this great work to the desperately understaffed ranks of the clergy, the Church will become stagnant and lost in parochial bickering, and its true glory will never even be glimpsed in the world outside.

This is the life of the communicant member who takes his life seriously; regular worship, public and private; the practical expression of that worship in the generous giving of time, talents and money for the work of Christ at home and abroad; and the conduct of every department of life as is befitting to one who owes his first allegiance to Jesus Christ. More than anything else is the Church of England in need of men and women of this calibre, men and women who have glimpsed the vision and have steadily refused to ignore it, however great the temptations may be in the world outside, those who have knelt at the foot of the Cross and have received shelter, those who have met a Guide on the highway of life and have cast away their own uncertain charts for ever. Yours is a great and high calling, and our Lord's words are addressed to you: 'Ye are the light of the world. Let your light so shine before men that they may see your good works and glorify your Father which is in heaven.'

Further reading:

Voices in the Wilderness (John Bowdler, SCM).

Discuss:

How far is the Church thought relevant to life to-day?

Ought the Church to be more 'involved' in the life of the community?

ONE OF CHRIST'S FOLLOWERS—ST. FRANCIS

His Background

It is a very great help to us in our study of the Christian religion if we summarize the life of one of the most outstanding of the followers of Christ, who really tried to live the life that Christ taught as being the best.

He was the son of a wealthy draper. His father was a self-made man, what we should call nowadays an average churchman, respectful to what he called 'the gentry,' very proud of his son, who became the friend of their sons, and with his father's money made their lives gay with pleasure and dances. He was never really bad—just thoughtless, and the sight, for example, of unemployment and poverty hurt him very much.

Then war came. He went to the front and was taken prisoner. In the prison camp he became the life and soul of the party, though he very much longed for home and the beauty of his own country.

The Turning-point

The war ended and he returned home to a wild time of gaiety and drinking, and, as is so often the case, his health suffered and he had to go to bed. When he was getting better, with the aid of a stick he climbed to his favourite view to look on the beauty of the hills and the lovely plain beneath, but instead of reviving him it made him completely miserable, and, after that, there followed a long period during which he was alone. He took long walks alone; he made companions of the poor and the ill and forced himself to feel what they were suffering. Then one day he met face to face the one sight above all others that made him feel quite sick with loathing—a man whose flesh had been eaten away by a horrible disease. He turned to run away, and then, by a very great effort, he came back, put his arms round the man and kissed him and gave him all the money he had on him. That incident was the turning-point in the life of the draper's son. He gave away everything he had and gave himself to the outcast and the diseased.

Just outside the town where he lived was a little chapel which was falling down and completely uncared for. Into this tumble-down building the young man went to pray. One day he prayed these words: 'Great and glorious God, let Your light come into the darkness of my mind. May I in all things do only what is in accordance with Your Holy Will.' From that time onwards he lived only to serve Christ.

His father, an average churchman, who believed that religion was 'all right in its place,' was shocked at such extravagant devotion and enthusiasm and, furious that his money should be spent on beggars and the sick, he disowned him. The boy's former companions mocked him and called him a madman. For years we do not know for quite how long, he was alone, misunderstood, insulted, mocked at, and *all because he took Christ's words literally.*

But such absolute devotion to Christ in an uneasy world could not fail to win through, and the hard shell of a 'respectable religion' just cracked before that example. The boy preached in the streets of his own village. He was not very clever and he knew no theology; but his words were simple, they came from his heart and he believed them completely. He had something to say and he believed what he said—these are the two essentials (there are no others) of preaching.

The Spread of the Message

That man, of course, was St. Francis of Assisi, whose name we commemorate on 4 October in the Church's calendar. Within a few months, five thousand men had joined him; in a few years, more than twenty thousand. They spread into every country, even into this. What was known as 'the long cruel winter' of the twelfth century, the winter of wars and bloodshed, destruction and religious squabbling and persecution, gave way to the joys of spring—and Francis was that spring. Men full of fear looked up again and were not afraid, and hope and courage returned because, out of that little man of Assisi, was born the greatest religious revival of all time, and also the Renaissance itself. The life of a town, a country, of Europe, was changed—*because one man took Christ's words literally.*

The Perennial Appeal of St. Francis

Why did and does this little draper's son of Assisi appeal to us so much? Surely it is because, in the first place, the age in which we live, like that of St. Francis, has worshipped material things—security and comfort and our pleasure and avoidance of suffering and the uncomfortable. *Things* have ruled our lives—and especially money and all that it brings, but really if we think at all about the state of the world to-day we must realize that these things are not the best. They fail to satisfy us. We want more—fellowship and friendship and gaiety and laughter and simple things; above all we want a *purpose,* something to live for and surrender to and be used by. If we are going to live to serve ourselves we shall be utterly miserable, and we see in Francis the joy of fellowship with religion at its heart and a high purpose in front. Can you describe the urgent need of our day better than that?

There was a cartoon which appeared at the end of the last war and which appealed to me, showing a man entering a train and speaking to a passenger who was obviously something 'big' in the city, and the passenger answering, 'How dare you speak to me, sir, there is no air raid on now!' And that is it; for suffering and danger brought us great fellowship at that time; and I know of no power, except the Christian religion, which can bind us together and give us this fellowship for ever.

Again we find the appeal of St. Francis was strong because he would not *alter his ideals.* In the end, the movement begun by Francis did compromise—the Church of that day forced it to. In the end the Church made the Franciscans accept a rule of life that

Francis had rejected. The movement ran to seed, but it remains a fact in history that it was the absoluteness and refusal to compromise of Francis that saved Christendom in Europe and lit a fire which has never been extinguished.

The one quality in Francis which includes all others, was the quality of sharing love with people, and it was his love of Jesus which made him love men so much. Position, wealth, learning—Francis had none of these things; he had only a single-hearted love for Christ which overflowed into love for men, and with that love alone he changed Europe. Out of this love sprang joy. Francis made it a rule of life that his followers must be joyful: 'Let the Brothers be careful not to show themselves outwardly miserable or gloomy hypocrites, but rather let them appear rejoicing in the Lord and gay and joyful and faithful.' The story of the early Franciscan movement is the story of shouts of laughter as they journeyed, healed and preached—possessing nothing. This joy came from communion with God and from communion with nature. They gave away money and possessions and security; and yet they were richer than ever before.

At the end, heartbroken by the Church's handling of the 'Little Brothers,' nearly blind, suffering intense agony from the disease which killed him, Francis could still, out of the joy that was in him, compose that famous 'Canticle to the Sun,' the oldest surviving poem in any modern language. A year later he died.

A Lay Movement

The last mark of Francis and his movement that I want you clearly to understand is that it was a lay one. Despite his sainthood and the fact that Francis was the greatest figure in the Church of the thirteenth century, he would not be ordained to the priesthood. It was what we should call a 'working class movement.' Francis insisted on his followers plying a trade, and wherever they worked with other men they preached—though more often by example than by word. Francis realized that the Church of his day was unfaithful to her mission, choked with wealth and corruption and bitter feuds, lost in ceremonial; *but though all his life he had to struggle against the Church from within, yet all his life he fought for the Church, seeking to purge and reform it.* A movement which might have split the Church asunder saved it and became its glory. How many of us could combine such intense enthusiasm and devotion for reform with such great patience and humility?

The world in which we find ourselves to-day is not so very different in its illnesses from the world of St. Francis. And there is to-day a mass of ignorance of the elements of the Christian faith, widespread indifference to religion, in some cases active hostility to the Church because it does not seem necessary. Regular worship and daily prayer are confined to less than five per cent of the people, and many outsiders tend to think that the things that the clergy say are only said because it is their job to say them.

It seems to me that the true answer to the desperate need nowadays is to be found somewhere in the answer given by Francis—the form may be entirely different, but the spirit must be the same. The making of a Christian Britain can never come through the clergy alone, and it is cowardly on the part of Churchmen who think that it may. Above all we need a Christian lay movement, a Christian lay order if you like, of men and women living by rule. Their marks will be the same—refusal to compromise, absolute love, gaiety and joy, utter surrender, a rule of life. They will purge, criticize, even oppose, the Church; but above all they will love and serve Her. What a vision for us to have before us, because if this really took root, anything less than the best in our religion would be unthinkable. Then, in us, men would see the joy of fellowship, with religion at its heart, and a high purpose in front; and if men once really see that they will respond; because that is man's greatest need and his assured destiny.

Further reading:

Any book on St. Francis of Assisi.

Discuss:

'If men see in us the joy of fellowship, with religion at its heart and a high purpose in front, they will respond.'

What is required of Christian laity to-day?

LIVING BY RULE

As a footnote to all that has been said here, it must be stressed that it is essential, if we are to make the best kind of progress in the Religious Life, that we have a rule about it. In the realm of physical life, any doctor will testify to the necessity of a regular diet. To live for most of the time on little or no food, but to indulge at irregular and rare intervals in large and heavy meals does not bring about good health. Many who recognize that this is true of one's physical life do not see that it is true also of the spiritual life. To ignore God for most of the time, saying prayers only in time of emergency, and visiting God's House 'when the spirit moves' is, to say the least, not a way likely to strengthen the soul. We all need a Rule of Life to keep us up to the mark, and it should be practical in its nature and one we are able to keep. Might I outline to you a simple Christian Rule of Life which may well be commended to all newly confirmed as an essential first step in our advance to a deepened spiritual fellowship? There are six parts to it and it is very simple:

(1) *To pray to God every day;* and remember that we may pray to God in any place. Brother Lawrence shows from his life that he was as conscious of the presence of God in his kitchen, where he was a monastery scullion, as he was when kneeling before the altar in the monastery chapel. Certainly never let a day pass without lifting up the heart and mind to God in prayer.

(2) *To worship every Sunday.* This is a great privilege and duty of which you may or may not be worthy.

(3) *To receive the Holy Communion every Sunday.* Around your attendance at this Sacrament hinges the whole of your spiritual life.

(4) *To read the Holy Bible regularly.* Here is the Word of God to men. As the Archbishop said to the Queen at her coronation, 'Here is the Royal Law.' Read a few verses regularly, preferably before your prayers, and, if you desire help in your reading, join the Bible Reading Fellowship, which gives excellent guidance in its monthly notes. Do not make the mistake of trying to read too much at a time. Sometimes two or three verses can give you a wealth of insight into the things of the spirit.

(5) *To perform at least one kind and unselfish action every day.* At the end of each day, look back and see if you have kept this apparently simple resolve. Try not only to do kind actions but to say kind things about others, and leave unsaid the unkind and censorious words, even though you might have longed to say them. This resolve may be the hardest of all to keep.

(6) *To give adequately of time, energy, and money for the continuance of the Church's work.* Every parish offers rich scope for the witnessing Christian to offer up talents, time and money. It is a question for your own conscience, and if you are merely content to give to God what you think you will not miss, the Church will not get on very quickly. Giving what one will not miss just will not do. If a man or woman is spending more on tobacco or cosmetics, on pictures or holiday jaunts, this gives that person's estimate of religion in a nutshell. One of the great values of the stewardship scheme at work in many parishes to-day is that one puts by a considered sum of money each week, and that is regarded as absolutely sacred and untouchable for any other purpose.

This, then, is an outline of a simple Rule of Life for you all. If you have no such rule, pray that God will give you the mind and will to make such a forward stride in your spiritual life. Those living by such a rule really mean business and, though at first it may seem drudgery, its ultimate rewards will be tremendous. Think what a change in our Church life if we all tried to put into practice the six points outlined!

APPENDIX III

MORNING PRAYERS

Remember that you are in God's presence. He loves you. He is listening now, as you come to Him in prayer. At your Baptism you were signed with the Cross in the name of the Most Holy Trinity. So it is good to begin your prayer:

✝ In the Name of the Father, and of the Son, and of the Holy Ghost. Amen.

An Act of Worship

O My God, I worship Thee,
  Who art so great and holy,
Help me now to lift my heart to Thee
  In love and praise.
Glory be to Thee, O Lord.

Thanksgiving

God has kept you safe through the night. He has given you all the happy things of your life. He gives you this new day in which to serve Him, and to show Him your love.

O Heavenly Father,
I thank Thee for all Thy love to me,
  For Thy gift of this new day.
I thank Thee, above all, for the knowledge of Thyself,
  And of Jesus Thy dear Son, our Saviour.
Thanks be to Thee, O Lord.

A Prayer for To-day

Think of the Lord Jesus, whom you promised at Baptism to serve. Think of all the brave Saints who have followed Him faithfully, and now pray for us in Heaven.

O Holy Jesu, most merciful Redeemer,
  Friend and Brother,
May I know Thee more clearly,
  Love Thee more dearly,
And follow Thee more nearly.

(St. Richard of Chichester, A.D. 1253)

Or think how the Lord Jesus, your King, calls you to-day to fight for Him on the side of all that is pure and true. Pray the Holy Spirit, whom Jesus promised to send to His Church, to help you to be faithful.

O HOLY SPIRIT, Who art one in love and glory
With the Father and the Son,
Help me to-day to do my duty.
Keep me true to-day to Jesus, my King.

Pray for Others

Remember those you love; all whom you will meet to-day, those who have hard things to face to-day; those living without God and the Lord Jesus. Pray for them all:

OUR FATHER, who art in heaven,
Hallowed be Thy Name,
Thy kingdom come,
Thy will be done,
On earth, as it is in heaven.
Give us this day our daily bread;
And forgive us our trespasses,
As we forgive those who trespass against us.
And lead us not into temptation,
But deliver us from evil. Amen.

DURING THE DAY

Try to remember God at least once during the day. We can send up to Him an arrow prayer anywhere, at any moment, such as:

DEAR LORD JESUS, keep me close to Thee.

At midday we might remember how the Lord Jesus said:

I, if I be lifted up from the earth, will draw all men unto me.

EVENING PRAYERS

Remember that you are in God's presence. To begin a prayer is like opening a door into heaven.

✝ In the Name of the Father, and of the Son, and of the Holy Ghost. Amen.

An Act of Worship

With Angels and with the whole company of heaven, adore the one, true, living God.

HOLY, HOLY, HOLY, Lord God of Hosts,
Heaven and earth are full of Thy Glory.
Glory be to Thee, O Lord most high.

Or You Can Make an Act of Faith

I BELIEVE in Thee, O GOD THE FATHER, who hast made me and all the world. All love, all glory be to Thee. I BELIEVE in Thee, O GOD THE SON, who hast redeemed me and all mankind. All love, all glory be to Thee. I believe in Thee, O GOD THE HOLY GHOST, who sanctifiest me and all the elect people of God. All love, all glory be to Thee.

Thanksgiving

Think of all that you owe to God to-day, and through all your life. Thank Him for the good news of the gospel, and for the blessings He gives you through His Holy Catholic Church.

GLORY be to the Father, and to the Son, and to the Holy Ghost: as it was in the beginning, is now, and ever shall be, world without end. Amen.

Penitence

Think whether you have failed Jesus, your Lord, to-day in thought, word or deed.

LORD JESU, I am truly sorry
For all the ways in which I disappoint Thy love,
I do want to love Thee truly.
Help me to begin afresh to serve and follow Thee.

Prayer for Others

Remember your home and church and work; all who work for us and guard us; all in danger of body or soul to-night. Say for them all:

OUR FATHER . . .

Pray that God's kingdom of truth and love may spread through all the world.

O HEAVENLY FATHER,
May Thy kingdom come
In my heart and home,
In all our land,
Through all the world.

The Peace of God

Remember that God keeps you, through His Holy Spirit, by day and night; that you are not alone, but one of God's great family in earth and heaven. Remember the dead who rest in Jesus.

DEAR GOD, keep me safe this night: and may the souls of the faithful rest in peace. ✝

APPENDIX IV

A SUMMARY OF THE FAITH

I. *God's Plan*

In the Apostles' Creed we say: 'I believe in God the Father Almighty, Maker of Heaven and earth.' God made you. He made you a person, different from every other person, because He has *special work* which He wills to do *through you,* in your home, at your work, or elsewhere. He has a purpose, a *plan* for *you.*

II. *Prayer*

God made you to *know Him,* to *love Him,* and to *serve Him* in this world; and to be *happy with Him* for ever hereafter. He *cares for you,* and His heart longs for you to come to know Him and to love Him. The best way of coming to know God is by *prayer.* Prayer does not merely mean 'asking for things.' Prayer means 'lifting up the heart and mind to God.' You need not use many words in your prayers. Every morning, *offer* yourself to God for the day; ask Christ to *use you* all day in His service. Every evening, *thank* God for His goodness to you; ask Him to forgive you *your sins* of thought, word, and deed committed during the day; and pray for other people.

III. *Sin*

Sin is *disobedience* to God, disloyalty to Him. Sin wounds the loving Heart of God. Sin interferes with God's plan for the world (e.g., War is a result of sin). The root of sin is *self-will,* to prefer your own way to God's will. You can sin in three ways: by *thought,* by *word,* and by *deed.*

IV. *Christ*

In the *Old Testament,* God teaches us about Himself, and we see how He prepared the world for the *coming of His Son.* In the *New Testament,* we read how God showed Himself to men as *Jesus Christ.* Jesus is not only man, but He is also *Almighty God.* In the Nicene Creed we say that *Jesus* is 'God of God, Light of Light, Very God of Very God. . . . Who for us men, and for our salvation came down from heaven, and was *incarnate* by the *Holy Ghost* of the *Virgin Mary,* and was made Man.' Jesus Christ had no human father (Matt. 1: 18–20; Luke 1: 35).

V. *The Cross*

To *save us* from the punishment which our sins deserve, the Son of God was crucified for us. On the *Cross,* He paid the price of our sins. Christians, therefore, are thankful for the Cross. When they are baptized they are signed on the forehead with the *sign of the Cross.* If the Cross of Christ is to save *you,* you must receive the Spirit of *Christ Crucified* into your heart. In the *Sacrament of Penance* (when Absolution is given after confession), the *Crucified Jesus* will come into your heart to wash away your sins.

VI. *The Resurrection and Ascension*

On the third day, the first *Easter Sunday,* our Lord *rose from the dead,* leaving an empty tomb (John 20).

Forty days later, on the first *Ascension Day,* 'He *ascended into heaven,* and sitteth on the right hand of God the Father Almighty' (Acts 1: 9). He had promised that He would send His Holy Spirit upon His Church, and that He would Himself come again (John 14: 16–18).

VII. *The Holy Ghost*

The Holy Spirit is the *'Lord and giver of Life.'* At the first Whitsun He came down to dwell in the *Church,* as Christ had promised (Acts 2: 1–4). He *lives and works* in and through the *Church.*

VIII. *The Catholic Church*

The *One, Holy, Catholic, Apostolic Church* was founded by Jesus Christ to carry on *His work* (*'Catholic'* means 'universal, for *all* people'). The Church of England is part of the Catholic Church. All baptized persons who have received the Spirit belong to the Church. The faithful *dead* are also members of the Church. We believe in the *'Communion of Saints,'* the fellowship in the Church of all faithful Christians living and dead.

IX. *The Creeds*

As our Lord promised, the *Holy Spirit guides the Church* 'into all truth' (John 16: 13). *Through His Church, Christ* speaks to us. The Holy Spirit has led the Church to believe in three Creeds: the Apostles' Creed, the Nicene Creed (recited at Holy Communion), and the Athanasian Creed. These Creeds are to be found in the Book of Common Prayer.

X. *The Ministry*

In the Church, there is a Ministry of three Orders: *Bishops, priests,* and *deacons.* Christ gives to each Order special work to do for Him, e.g., to *bishops* He gives authority to *ordain* and to *confirm;* to *priests* He gives authority to *celebrate Communion* and to *forgive sins* in His name.

XI. *Grace and the Sacraments*

Because you are weak, God offers to you *His help, His power,* commonly called *'grace.'* Without grace, you can achieve nothing. The *Sacraments* are *means of grace,* 'outward and visible signs of an inward and spiritual grace' (Prayer Book Catechism). They are ways in which *Jesus* comes to you to help you. There are *seven Sacraments* of the Church. Two of these are *'generally necessary to salvation,* that is to say, Baptism and the Supper of the Lord' (Catechism).

(i) In *Baptism,* the *Spirit* comes to you, *Christ Himself* is born in you, you become a 'member of Christ.' Jesus said: 'Except a man be born of water and of the Spirit, he cannot enter into the kingdom of God' (John 3: 5).

(ii) In *Holy Communion, Jesus* gives you *His Body* and *Blood* (under the forms of bread and wine). As He gives you earthly food chiefly for the good of your body, so He gives you this *heavenly Food* chiefly for the good of your *soul.* Jesus said: 'Except ye *eat the flesh* of the Son of Man, and *drink his blood,* ye have *no life* in you' (John 6: 53).

(iii) *Confirmation* is a gift of the *Spirit,* given to you by the laying on of a bishop's hands, to *strengthen* you to fight against evil and to do good (Acts 8: 14–17).

(iv) In the Sacrament of *Penance, Absolution* is given by a priest to those who have confessed their sins, and are truly sorry for them, and mean to do better in the future. Christ gave to His Church authority to forgive sins in His name: 'Whose soever sins ye remit, they are remitted unto them: and whose soever sins ye retain, they are retained' (John 20: 23).

(v) In *Ordination,* through the laying on of a bishop's hands, the Spirit is given to those who are thus made *bishops, priests,* or *deacons,* to help them to do God's work in the Church.

(vi) In *Holy Matrimony,* God joins a man and a woman together as husband and wife, and gives them grace to be faithful to each other, and to bring up their children as good Christians.

(vii) In *Holy Unction,* grace is given to a sick or dying person through an anointing with holy oil.

XII. *The Holy Communion*

This is the *Lord's Service,* which Jesus instituted in the Upper Room on the night before He died. He said: *'Do this in remembrance of me'* (Luke 19: 19–20; 1 Cor. 11: 23–6). This Service is sometimes called the 'Eucharist,' or the 'Mass.' The Church of England directs her confirmed members to receive Communion at least 'three times in the year, of which Easter Day is to be one' (Book of Common Prayer). In the Service:

(i) Bread and wine are *offered* to God (at the Offertory).

(ii) They are changed by Him into the *Body and Blood of Christ* (at the Consecration).

(iii) The one, perfect, holy Sacrifice of the *Body and Blood of Christ* is *offered* to God 'for us men and for our salvation,' 'for the sins of the whole world,' for the living and the dead.

(iv) The Body and Blood of Christ are received by the priest and people, and eaten and drunk (at the *Communion*). Every Christian ought to be present at the Lord's Service at least on Sunday mornings and on great festivals of the Church.

XIII. *The Body of Christ*

As the same blood flows in all the different parts of a human body, so the same *Spirit* lives in all baptized members of the *Church*. They are *'members of Christ,'* and the Church is the *'Body of Christ.'* Each member of the Church has *special work* to do for the *Body of Christ,* as the eye or the ear has special work to do for the human body (Rom. 12: 4–5). You must let the Spirit freely live and work in you, so that men may see *Christ* acting and hear Him speaking *through you* as a member of His Body. They ought to be able to see the *'fruit of the Spirit'* growing in you (who have received the Spirit). St. Paul wrote: 'The fruit of the Spirit is love, joy, peace, longsuffering, gentleness, goodness, faith, meekness, temperance.' The Spirit in you will give you the help you need to keep the two great commandments of Jesus: 'Thou shalt love the Lord thy God with all thy heart,' and 'Thou shalt love thy neighbour as thyself.'

XIV. *Judgment and Life after Death*

After death, *Christ* will *judge* you. 'From thence he shall come to judge both the quick and the dead.' Your life in this world determines your fate after death.

(i) *Hell.* Those who deliberately reject and rebel against God cut themselves off from Him, and condemn themselves to Hell.

(ii) *Heaven.* Those who are perfect, the saints, are fit for Heaven, where they 'see God face to face.' Our Lord said: 'Blessed are the pure in heart: for they shall see God.'

(iii) *The Intermediate State.* Those who are imperfect, but who have not hated or utterly rejected God, do not go to Hell, but to an *intermediate state,* sometimes called Paradise. There the soul is cleansed from sin. We must *pray for the dead* in Paradise, that God may give them rest and light and peace.

XV. *The Life Everlasting*

As Christ rose from the dead on Easter Day, so we too hope to rise. We believe in the Resurrection of the body, and the Life everlasting.' The 'new body' with which we hope to rise will be a transformed and glorious body.

APPENDIX V

A TYPICAL 'FAMILY TREE' SHOWING THE ORGANIZATION OF THE CHURCH OF ENGLAND IN RELATION TO THE WHOLE CHURCH

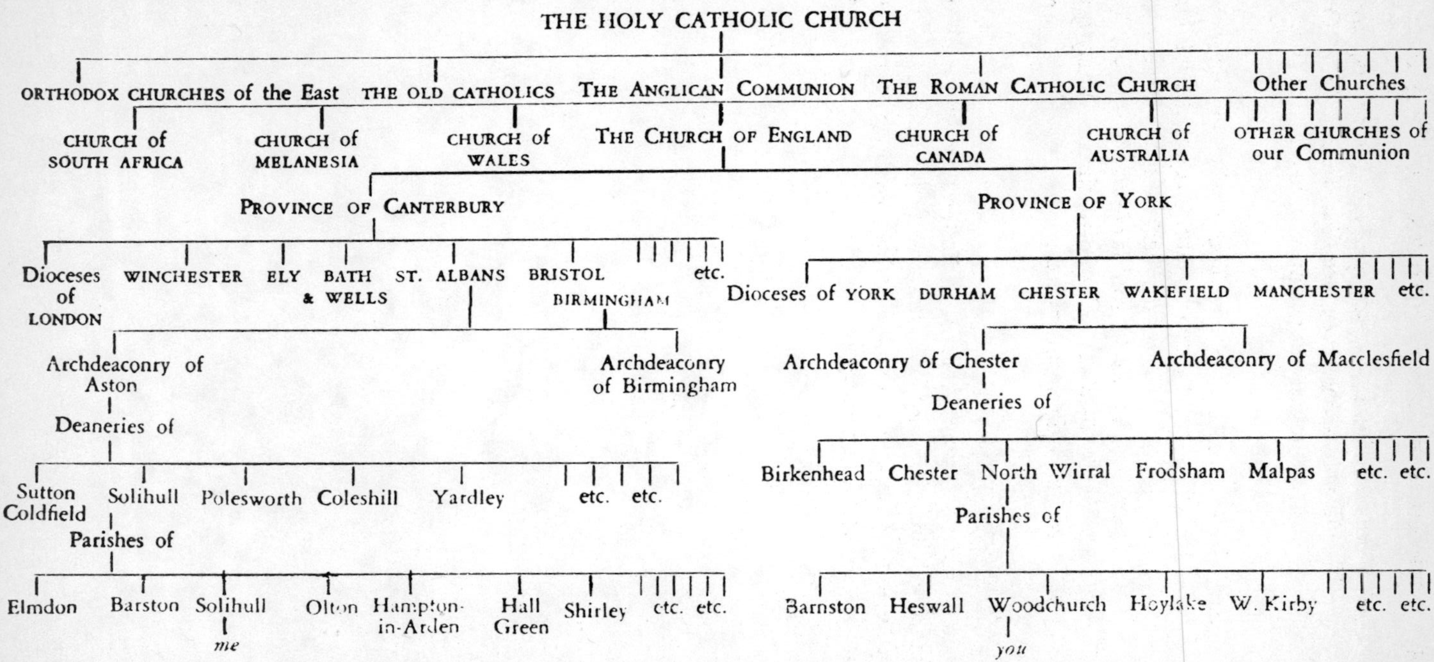

Thus, every one in this country belongs to a parish, which is part of a deanery, which is part of an archdeaconry, which is part of a diocese, which is part of a province, which is part of the Church of England, which is part of the Anglican Communion, which is part of the Holy Catholic Church.